HARLEM IN THE TWENTIETH CENTURY

Noreen Mallory

Published by The History Press
Charleston, SC 29403
www.historypress.net

Copyright © 2011 by Noreen Mallory
All rights reserved

Cover photos courtesy of Jamel Shabazz (front, top right and back, left) and
the Library of Congress.
Unless otherwise noted, all images are from the author's collection.

First published 2011

Manufactured in the United States

ISBN 978.1.59629.651.0

Library of Congress Cataloging-in-Publication Data
Mallory, Noreen.
Harlem in the twentieth century / Noreen Mallory.
p. cm.
Includes bibliographical references.
ISBN 978-1-59629-651-0
1. Harlem (New York, N.Y.)--History--20th century. 2. Harlem (New York, N.Y.)--Social
conditions--20th century. 3. New York (N.Y.)--History--20th century. 4. New York (N.Y.)--
Social conditions--20th century. I. Title.
F128.68.H3M27 2011
974.7'1044--dc23
2011043443

Notice: The information in this book is true and complete to the best of our knowledge. It is offered without guarantee on the part of the author or The History Press. The author and The History Press disclaim all liability in connection with the use of this book.

All rights reserved. No part of this book may be reproduced or transmitted in any form whatsoever without prior written permission from the publisher except in the case of brief quotations embodied in critical articles and reviews.

For Averlyn, friend and devoted champion of the Harlem arts community

CONTENTS

Introduction	7
Harlem History Since 1900	11
The People of Harlem	35
Foods and Flavors of Harlem	87
Cultural Crusades: From Jazz to Hip-Hop	90
Faith and Religion in the Community	99
Tourists and Transitions	103
Harlem Now	110
Notes	121
Bibliography	125
About the Author	127

INTRODUCTION

Harlem, New York. From the moment one hears these words, the illustrious history of one of America's most famous neighborhoods comes to mind. Culturally rich and vibrant, Harlem is most known for the Harlem Renaissance of the 1920s and 1930s. But just as Harlem was dynamic and changing throughout the early twentieth century, it continues to change today. And ever since the city of New York was first settled by the Dutch, Harlem would transform again and again over the years, establishing itself as one of the most dynamic communities in the United States.

In the late eighteenth century, the Harlem area first gained historical notoriety during the Revolutionary War. In 1776, General George Washington and the Continental army fought British troops at the Battle of Harlem Heights. Today, a bronze and granite marker sits in Harlem's Riverside Park commemorating the event. However, much of the area where the Revolutionary War events took place is north of what is now considered Harlem, in what is now called Washington Heights.

Nieuw Haarlem, as it was called by the Dutch in the early 1600s, was once a massive area of farmland occupied by American Indians and later settled by the Dutch in 1658. The Dutch East India Company led exploration of the area by commissioning early exploring expeditions. One of the first people to lead one of these expeditions was the English explorer Henry Hudson, who was hired by the Dutch East India Company to find a new sea route to the East—and whose name would eventually become so much a part of New York history that a river, a street and countless businesses would use "Hudson" in their company names. Walk anywhere in New York City and

Introduction

you will undoubtedly see "Hudson" posted on a building or rolling by on the side of a commercial vehicle.

From its very beginning, this part of New York City just above Central Park was changing and developing constantly. When Dutch explorers reached the area, American Indians were the only people settled there. As the Dutch first began to establish farming settlements in New York during the 1600s, it set the stage for the beginning of one of the most influential communities in New York City and the United States. From its beginnings as a farming community, Nieuw Haarlem would ultimately become a place where New York's wealthy and well-off acquired and maintained expansive homes.

American Indians and then the Dutch and the English were the early occupants of this part of North Manhattan. Over the years and decades, Harlem would go through transitions, and Irish, Jewish and Italian residents would all call Harlem home before World War I and the Great Migration. After the war and throughout the migration, thousands of African Americans moved from the South to various cities in the North—Philadelphia, Chicago, Detroit—in search of jobs and better opportunities. In New York City, Harlem is where they headed. And as African Americans rushed to Harlem, Latinos from the Caribbean were also making their way to New York City. In 1900, half of the more than 7,500 Latin Americans in New York City were immigrants from the Caribbean.

African Americans continued to flock to Harlem in large numbers after World War I and through the 1920s and 1930s during Harlem's most well-known period—the Harlem Renaissance. The energy that drew creative types—writers, musicians, actors and actresses—also brought black professionals, teachers, doctors and lawyers. In 1910, the 90,000 Negroes in New York represented less than 2 percent of the population. By 1920, their numbers had increased to 150,000, or about 3 percent. Before the end of the 1920s, the Negro population more than doubled, leaping to 327,000. Most of them wound up in Harlem, which became a city within a city and the Negro capital of the world.[1]

The Harlem Renaissance of the 1920s and 1930s is probably the most recognized period in Harlem history. During these years, some of America's literary and artistic canons surged onto the scene. From poets to painters to musicians, Harlem was the place to be, especially for African American artists. Langston Hughes, Zora Neale Hurston, James Weldon Johnson, Duke Ellington and countless others called Harlem home. The cultural renaissance and the explosion of jazz were Harlem phenomena that attracted worldwide attention.[2]

Introduction

During the middle of the century, the 1940s, 1950s and 1960s, Harlem's political traditions began to take firm root. This was also the time that Harlem's reputation as an entertainment mecca soared. People traveled across the country and abroad to go to the theater, wine, dine and dance "uptown"—a name that is still often applied to Harlem. Celebrities made Harlem a regular stop; some called Harlem home. However, as whites traveled from downtown New York and beyond, the racism that dominated the American South became much more visible in Harlem. After the Great Migration and the Harlem Renaissance, the ugly face of racism and segregation began to show more frequently in housing, jobs and even entertainment. And as Harlem's nightclubs became more popular and drew more whites, most were off-limits to blacks. As an oppressive society magnified, Harlem would respond.

The early decades of the twentieth century—the 1920s and 1930s—were transformational in many ways for Harlem. These were the years that helped establish Harlem's social reputation and artistic glory. However, during the later years—the 1950s and 1960s—Harlem also established itself solidly as the pulse of the black community, not just in New York but all of America. If you wanted to know what black folks were thinking, feeling or experiencing, one of the first places you would go is Harlem, New York. Numerous iconic political and religious figures for African Americans emerged during these years. They would go on to develop national and worldwide reputations and become familiar names in the annals of American history.

The middle and later years of the century would see Harlem fall to the same ills that hit many other urban communities in America—racial oppression and discrimination, job loss, drugs and crime. At one time during the 1970s, the City of New York owned about 70 percent of the housing stock in Harlem. However, Harlem has shown its resiliency over the years. The creative energy that launched the Harlem Renaissance has remained a constant. Those in the arts continue to be drawn to Harlem from all over the world, and they arrive in droves each year. Today, Harlem remains a cultural and artistic hotbed.

It is hard to imagine any other place in America that has as extraordinary a history as Harlem, New York. Harlem would experience the splendor of the Harlem Renaissance, the devastation of several race riots, the massive influx of new residents during the Great Migration, the impact of poverty and economic slowdown and yet consistently produce some of the most powerful and influential people in America. Politicians, Supreme Court justices, historians, artists, writers, Olympians and even former presidents

Introduction

A neighborhood block of one of Harlem's historic brownstone homes. Most of these homes were built in the late nineteenth century.

and presidential cabinet members have all lived or worked in Harlem, New York.

Today, Harlem is changing again. A new influx of people is moving to the community. New housing is being developed. Big business, which once shunned the area, is taking a foothold. Tourists make Harlem a regular stop. Yes, Harlem is changing again. Many people seem to be thinking along the lines of that famous song lyric, "Take me to Harlem…"

Getting to Harlem is easy. Buttressed between the Hudson River to the west and the Harlem River to the east, Harlem begins near the top of Central Park around 110th Street and extends east and west up to about 155th Street. All of the major subway lines running through Manhattan stop in Harlem. The A, B, C or D trains and the #1 train will drop you off on the west side of Harlem. For Central Harlem and the Lenox Avenue area, the #2 and #3 trains will get you there. And for the east side of Harlem and Spanish Harlem or "El Barrio," the 4, 5 and 6 trains are your best bet. Get more info at www.mta.info. In the meantime, take the advice of legendary band leader Duke Ellington and "take the 'A' Train" and head "uptown"!

HARLEM HISTORY SINCE 1900

The early twentieth century in Harlem was an era of constant change and shifting populations. Originally settled by the Dutch and English, Jews and Italians lived in Harlem before African Americans migrated in large numbers from the South. It is interesting now, more than one hundred years later, to note the similarities today to Harlem of yesteryear. In the early 1900s, housing and transportation were major developmental issues in Harlem. Beginning in the late nineteenth century, the expansion of some railroads and planned expansion of others into Harlem spurred new housing development. Harlem life altered radically in the first decade of the twentieth century. The construction of new subway routes into the neighborhood in the late 1890s set off a second wave of speculation in Harlem land and property.[3]

Tenements and apartments were rapidly being built in anticipation of an impending boom. However, Harlem had been isolated and neglected for years near the end of the nineteenth century. This, along with many other factors, drastically changed Harlem's future. Nowadays, there is a resurgence of speculation and anticipation about Harlem. Housing development is occurring throughout the area, and new people are moving in. In several years, a new subway—the Second Avenue line—will open on the east side of Harlem. This is a much-anticipated addition that will ease overcrowding on some of the other subway lines while simultaneously making access to a rejuvenated East Harlem easier and quicker.

The most important factor underlying the establishment of Harlem as a Negro community was the substantial increase of Negro population in New York City in the years 1890 to 1914. By 1910, there were 91,709 Negroes in the metropolis, the majority southern-born.[4] Between 1920 and 1930, the number

Macombs Dam Bridge is a swing bridge that crosses the Harlem River. It is the third oldest bridge in New York City and was named a landmark in 1992.

of blacks in Harlem increased by 120,000 (to more than 200,000), while the number of whites decreased by an equivalent amount. Most of the new black residents were from the American South.[5] However, the wave of African Americans—or Negroes, as they were called during those years—was not the first to call Harlem home. The first Negroes to live and work in Harlem were slaves, and references to them are found in seventeenth-century documents. Slaves worked on farms and estates in Harlem in the seventeenth and eighteenth centuries, and colonial Harlem even had its own "Negro Burying Ground."[6] Ironically, from a beginning where blacks were slaves in Harlem, eventually the very same part of Manhattan—Harlem—would become the apex of African American life. And African Americans would excel in this new apex, as many would go on to become the "first African American" to achieve in a variety of their chosen fields. This included men as well as women.

One woman who defied obstacles and shattered limitations was none other than Ms. Sarah Breedlove, more commonly known as Madame C.J. Walker. The name Madame C.J. Walker comes from Breedlove's second husband, Charles Joseph Walker, a newspaperman whom she married in Denver, Colorado, and with whom she would eventually start her manufacturing

The grave of Madame C.J. Walker.

company. Although they divorced after several years of marriage, she continued using the name. Like a number of other African American women who achieved great success during the early twentieth century, Breedlove struggled with personal obstacles during the early part of her life. However, she would eventually make her way to Harlem and become one of the most influential and inspiring women of her day.

Sarah Breedlove was born in 1867 on a cotton plantation near Delta, Louisiana, to parents Owen and Minerva Breedlove, who were slaves. The couple died in 1874 from yellow fever. Orphaned at seven years old, Sarah and her older sister worked in Vicksburg, Mississippi cotton fields to survive.

Sarah Breedlove, or Madame C.J. Walker, as she would become known, also worked as a laundress before she discovered a hair-straightening process called the "Walker system," which made her a fortune. She ultimately became the first female millionaire in the United States. She would enjoy her rewards, too, and in 1913, she built a mansion for herself on West 136th Street and four years later built a magnificent country estate, Villa Lewaro, in exclusive Irvington-on-the-Hudson.[7]

Walker's impact on the black community was monumental in more ways than one. Not only did she amass her own fortune, but she also provided opportunity to thousands of African American women. Madame C.J. Walker created a school to teach women to be salespersons. At the time, it was virtually unheard of for this kind of opportunity to be provided for African American women.

Just as African Americans would eventually flock to Harlem, real estate speculation and the opportunities that come with a burgeoning community drew Jews to Harlem from New York's Lower East Side. In the section of Harlem north of Central Park to 125th Street and west of Lexington Avenue to Seventh Avenue, new tenements and apartment houses went up in the late 1890s. These properties seemed to offer "good profit on investments" as East European Jews spilled out of the Lower East Side in search of better homes—part of the migration to lower Harlem and other boroughs that reflected their economic mobility. The disintegration of the Jewish sections on the Lower East Side that began in the first decade of the twentieth century continued for thirty years.[8] However, years later, as sales of newly built brownstones in Harlem slowed down, one man would step in and literally create a new market based off this downward slide in sales.

Philip A. Payton Jr. was born in Westfield, Massachusetts. The son of a barber, Payton graduated from Livingston College in Salisbury, North Carolina, in 1898. The following year, he married and moved to New York seeking opportunity. Payton's arrival in New York in 1899 was during a boom atmosphere and speculative time in real estate—and he would soon jump in.

Working at several odd jobs, he found his passion while working as a janitor at a real estate company. At the turn of the century, at twenty-four years old, Payton decided to go into business for himself developing a specialized market that he singlehandedly created. Unsuccessful in the beginning, he was evicted from his own apartment and could not afford to pay for his office any longer. In fact, he would struggle for at least a year before getting a "colored tenement" to manage.

"My first opportunity came as a result of a dispute between two landlords in West 134th Street. To 'get even' one of them turned his house over to me to fill with colored tenants. I was successful in renting and managing this house and after a time I was able to induce other landlords to…give me their houses to manage."[9] Within a short time, Payton began to advertise his services in white real estate journals:

Colored Tenements Wanted
Colored man makes a specialty of managing colored
Tenements; references; bond. Philip A. Payton, Jr.,
agent and broker, 67 West 134th

In 1904, Payton founded the Afro-American Realty Company, which would become a crucial Harlem business responsible for making houses and apartments in Harlem available to numerous African Americans whom other realtors were not providing access to. He would soon become a respected figure in "Negro New York."

There were essentially two things that happened to set the stage for Harlem to become a sizeable African American community. In Manhattan, populations were already shifting across the island at the turn of the century. Jews were moving from the southern part of Manhattan uptown. And some whites who were already living in Harlem were not happy at any proposed or real change to their Harlem neighborhoods, and they attempted to block homeownership sales to African Americans. Often, Payton and the Afro-American Realty Company would step in.

The company had its genesis in a partnership of ten Negroes organized by Payton. This partnership specialized in acquiring five-year leases on Harlem property owned by whites and subsequently renting them to Negroes. The company was incorporated on June 15, 1904, and was permitted to "buy, sell, rent, lease and sublease, all kinds of buildings, houses…lots, and other…real estate in the City of New York."[10]

On the east side of Harlem, Puerto Ricans steadily began building New York City's most famous Latin American community. Beginning in the mid-nineteenth century, the neighborhood grew when the United States expanded trade in Latin America and the Caribbean. Puerto Ricans became the largest Latin American group in New York City by the early 1940s. Already accounting for 18 percent of the total Spanish-speaking population in 1920, they increased their share to 46 percent in 1940 and 81 percent by 1960; between 1940 and 1970, they grew in number from 61,463 to 811,843.[11]

One of the favorite sons of East Harlem (or, as it is commonly called, Spanish Harlem or El Barrio) is Ernest Anthony "Tito" Puente. Known as "El Rey" or the king of Latin jazz, Puente's family was one of the early Puerto Rican families arriving in New York City at the turn of the century. Tito Puente was born to Ernest and Ercilla on April 20, 1923, in Harlem Hospital and

Above left: Harlem fire station engine #37, located on 125th Street, bills itself as the "Heart of Harlem" in a colorful design on the station house door.

Above right: A 1940 article in the *New York Amsterdam News* chronicled the lives of Puerto Ricans living in Harlem.

grew up in Harlem, where, as a child, he began his illustrious musical career.

It was during World War I and the Great Migration —the period when African Americans from the South moved in great numbers to northern cities such as Boston, Philadelphia, Chicago and New York in search of better job opportunities and an overall better quality of life—that most African Americans flocked to Harlem. This included movement to Harlem from other parts of Manhattan.

Early 1900s East Harlem firehouse.

By 1917, when the United States was at war, there was an increased influx of blacks from the South and areas in the Caribbean into certain areas of Harlem. However, Harlem was by no means characterized as a black area of town. African Americans were scattered on various blocks extending from 130th to 140th Streets and between Fifth and Seventh Avenues in an area called the black belt. Whites occupied 130th Street down to 125th Street and below. Italians lived east of Fifth and as far south as Central Park North. The Irish and Jews occupied the areas west of Seventh Avenue.[12]

As America battled in World War I, soldiers based in Harlem, New York, would put their mark on history. Subjected to the second-class status that other non-military African Americans endured and were all too familiar with, a contingent of African American soldiers from Harlem's National Guard was organized. Officially, they were the 369th Regiment of the New York National Guard and the 15th Regiment of the New York Guard. In 1916, Harlem's National Guard unit, the "Fighting 15th" (later the 369th), was outfitted. Negroes had unsuccessfully requested a military organization for themselves since the Spanish-American War. Harlem's "Hell Fighters" made a distinguished record in France during World War I: the entire outfit was awarded the *Croix de Guerre* for bravery by the French government, and the 15th spent more days in combat

Early image of Harlem Hospital, where numerous well-known African Americans have been treated. Today, the hospital is located across the street from the Schomburg Center.

(191) than any other American unit. A "Happy Harlem," a "proud Harlem" greeted the soldiers on their return, and the 15th's exploits became part of the ghetto's folklore. In the 1920s, the largest National Guard armory in the state was constructed in Harlem for New York's "Black Watch."[13]

Today, the 369th Regiment Armory stands at 2360 Fifth Avenue and was designated a landmark in 1985. It is composed of two buildings built by two different architectural firms, a drill shed and an administration building and is one of the last armories built in New York City.

The Harlem Hellfighters made history collectively as a group, but individually they made history as well. Together, the units would serve again during World War II, where the 369th Coast Artillery (as it was redesignated in 1940) saw service in Okinawa, Japan, in 1945. The two units were renamed the 369th and the 870th Anti-Aircraft Artillery Battalions in 1943. The 369th Regiment of the New York National Guard would serve stateside during the Korean War in 1950. In 1974, it became the 369th Transportation Battalion. In 1990–91, both companies of the 369th served in the Persian Gulf and once again were recognized for their service and received the Meritorious Unit Citation.

Two people who served with the Harlem Hellfighters would go on to receive individual accolades both within and outside of the military. One would rise up in military ranks, and the other would forge two careers—a military service career and a continuing musical career.

Harlem History Since 1900

Harlem Hellfighters. *Courtesy of the National Archives.*

From 1936 to 1940, Colonel Benjamin O. Davis Sr. commanded the 369th Regiment. In 1940, he became the first African American military general. Another member of the 369th, James Reese Europe, achieved success prior to joining the 369th as well as after signing on with the unit. And he, too, experienced being a "first" achiever.

Born in Mobile, Alabama, and raised in Washington, D.C., James Reese Europe came to New York City in 1900. Here Europe, in his early twenties, almost immediately became professionally successful. He wrote some well-received songs and became a sought-after conductor of musical shows, working with Bert Williams, Bob Cole and others. In this era, the musicians' union in New York, Local 803 of the American Federation of Musicians, excluded African Americans. In response to this, in 1910, James Europe helped to create the Clef Club, an organization that provided black musicians with regular bookings and union-style benefits, such as insurance and unemployment relief.

Leading the group's flagship band, the Clef Club Orchestra, James Europe became one of the city's busiest and most successful conductors.

James Reese Europe.

Concerts in Carnegie Hall and other major venues brought the first dignified large-scale presentations of black popular music to the general public. His ragtime recordings displayed imaginative arrangements with colorful percussion effects, heavy use of violins and various exotic international styles. In 1913, Europe's group became the first all–African American band to be recorded by a commercial American label.[14]

James Reese Europe followed Scott Joplin in bringing ragtime music—a precursor to jazz—to the masses. His music became more successful at the time he joined the Harlem Hellfighters. He would be commissioned a captain and serve as the director to the Hellfighters' regimental band while at the same time maintaining leadership of his civilian Clef Club Orchestra.

Europe served in the military with another future bandleader, Noble Sissle. The two bandleaders would enjoy success in Harlem after the war; however, Sissle would enjoy it longer. After returning from France, the majority of the 369th Regiment survived and was welcomed home in great celebratory fashion. New Yorkers greeted them with a massive parade that turned into what could be called a good ole Harlem street party. Since Harlem is where Europe lived and worked, this would seem to be a fitting place to celebrate.

Unfortunately, as it turned out, it would also be one of the last mass celebrations Europe would be able to enjoy. In 1919, during a break in a performance with his Clef Club Orchestra, James Reese Europe was stabbed to death in his dressing room by a mentally unstable member of his band. His last major public event would be his funeral, which was held in New York City.

Although slavery was a thing of the past, remnants of the system were ever-present in New York life. One system of oppression ended while giving birth to its "sister in oppression"—Jim Crow. Racial tensions between different ethnic groups had been present to some degree since the late 1800s, but blacks in Harlem would experience several incidents throughout the 1900s that led to riots in the streets.

Throughout the twentieth century, Harlem would experience at least three significant race riots. Race and Harlem through the years is interesting because since its founding, Harlem has always had a sort of middle-of-the-road position on the racial map. When the Dutch first settled the area in 1658, black slaves were present. Later, free black farmers would remain in Harlem as some of the first homesteaders. During the 1920s through the 1940s, as Harlem became known for its arts and culture, nightlife and numerous clubs and theaters, there were certain dance clubs in Harlem where blacks and whites were always permitted to dance together—even when the rest of society's social mores dictated otherwise.

Throughout the first half of the twentieth century, several race riots exploded in Harlem and in many ways helped shift Harlem's reputation from one as primarily an arts and entertainment mecca to that of a political powerhouse. The combination effect of the Great Depression and the racial unrest over the years would have an enormous impact on the future of Harlem. After riots in 1935 followed a false rumor that a young boy caught stealing a penknife had been beaten to death and in 1943, after a white officer shot a black soldier, the people of Harlem were becoming more vocal and politically alive. Riots would erupt again in 1964 after the killing of a fifteen-year-old African American male by a white police officer.

In the 1950s and 1960s, the politics of civil and human rights on a scale much broader than just the Harlem community was taking root in Harlem. Issues particularly affecting African Americans throughout America were being shaped. And the number of people fighting for those rights who were based in Harlem increased too.

One of the leading organizations working for equal rights, the NAACP, was founded in New York City in February 1909. The National Association for the Advancement of Colored People led the fight in court seeking social change. During the '50s and '60s, future Supreme Court justice and Harlem resident Thurgood Marshall was still serving as an attorney for the

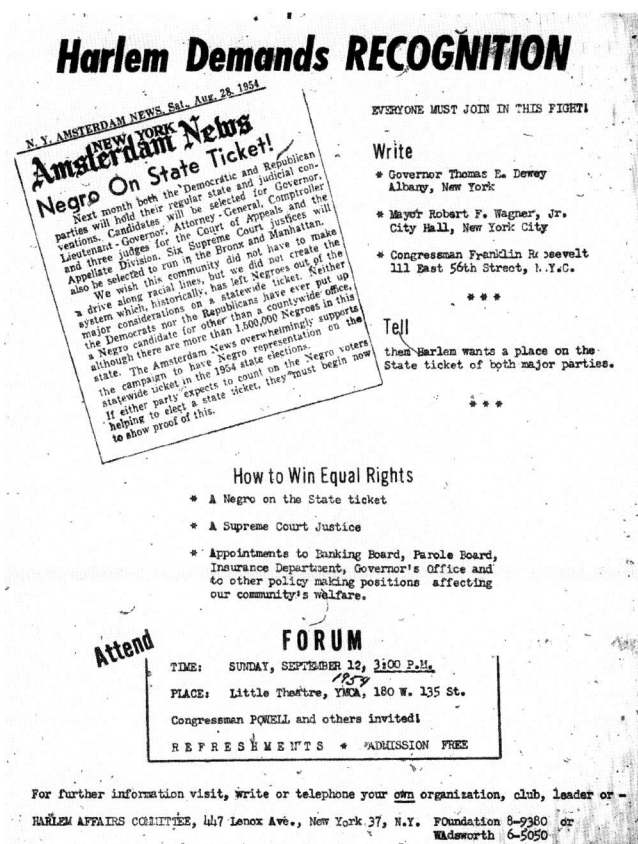

A 1954 political flyer urging Harlem residents to rally elected officials. Notice that the meeting is held at the landmark 135th Street YMCA.

NAACP. The NAACP's top lawyer was spending considerable time in the NAACP offices in consultation with his brilliant team of lawyers, historians and educators setting the strategy and calling the plays for the impending showdown with the Supreme Court. The 1954 *Brown* Supreme Court decision struck down for public education the "separate but equal" doctrine of *Plessy v. Ferguson*. The NAACP victory didn't abolish legal segregation in restaurants, hotels and parks, but it did send forth a signal.[15]

Marshall, the African American lawyer who led the fight in *Brown v. the Board of Education*, lived and socialized in Harlem. The future Supreme Court justice and many of his colleagues and fellow African American professionals and business owners maintained Harlem as a home base.

During the 1950s and 1960s, the foundation of the "black nationalist" and "black power" movements set in. Recognizable names from the African American struggle for civil rights emerged and flourished from Harlem

Harlem History Since 1900

Harlem's 125th Street today still shows signs of its activist past. Here, a man sits near photographs of slavery. Next to the pictures is the African American flag.

With his many accomplishments often overlooked, Paul Robeson was scorned because of his political views. He lived in Harlem and graduated from Columbia University Law School.

during these years. Stokely Carmichael, Harold Cruse, Amiri Baraka, Martin Luther King Jr. and Malcolm X all became leaders in the fight for civil rights during this time. Numerous other artists and activists emerged during this era.

Martin Luther King Jr. and Malcolm X would rise and become leading civil rights advocates, even as their own individual messages revealed contrasting ideologies. Both King and Malcolm X would spend a lot of time in Harlem spreading their individual messages of equality and justice to the people. Malcolm X would eventually lead one of the most recognized Islamic mosques in the country, Muhammad Mosque #7 in Harlem, which still remains in Harlem today at 106–8 West 127th Street.

There were many famous and not-so-famous people who canvassed Harlem with political messages. Harlem had always been active and politically vibrant, and King and Malcolm X were certainly two of the most dynamic leaders operating in Harlem's political community. But there were many whose names would emerge and become recognizable worldwide for their political activism, which for many had roots in Harlem.

The political movements of Harlem largely begun in the 1930s by Adam Clayton Powell Jr. and his father contributed to Harlem becoming a foundation for activism. This would be evident in not only politics but also the creative works coming from post–Renaissance era Harlem artists. Writer James Baldwin and playwright Lorraine Hansberry, the award-winning writer of the play *A Raisin in the Sun*, would emerge during these years.

Baldwin, who was born and raised in Harlem, would become a premier voice in the writing world who spoke poignantly about the racial and social climate of America. Some of his most notable works include *Go Tell It On the Mountain*, which was his first novel and an autobiographical work about growing up in Harlem; *Notes of a Native Son*, published in 1955; and *Giovanni's Room*, published in 1956. In 1963, Baldwin published *The Fire Next Time*, his highly acclaimed and powerful condemnation of racism in America.

As inspiring and creative as Harlem has been—and continues to be—it has certainly had its dark days. In its heyday between the 1920s and 1930s—the Prohibition era—Harlem was as known for its legitimate clubs and entertainment as it was for its illegal clubs and places to buy illegal alcohol. Speakeasies littered Harlem and were discreetly scattered about the neighborhood.

The latter decades of Harlem—after the civil rights movement—would see plight, a loss of jobs and housing and an upswing in crime. During part of the 1970s and 1980s, the City of New York owned a large percentage of Harlem's housing stock. The image of Harlem in these years is what contributed to the negative perception that was attached to Harlem for many years.

Landmarks

Known for its extraordinary history in politics, music and the arts, Harlem is also rich in architectural history and historic landmarks. Many may be familiar with Harlem as a neighborhood full of brownstones; however, throughout East and West Harlem, its intricate and ornate architecture extends from houses to community buildings to libraries, churches, schools, theaters, police stations and other structures such as historic street lampposts, which can be seen throughout different areas in New York City.

In the Hamilton Heights section of Harlem, a cast-iron twin lamppost dating back to the early twentieth century sits at the intersection of Amsterdam Avenue, Hamilton Place and West 143rd Street. The lamppost is one of nearly one hundred cast-iron lampposts in New York City that in 1997 were designated historic landmarks by the New York City Landmarks Preservation Commission. Another historic lamppost can be seen in Harlem at the entrance to Harlem River Drive at Adam Clayton Powell Jr. Boulevard.

Visitors to Harlem today can travel down the same streets where numerous cultural and political icons once lived and thrived. And along with hearing the stories of their fascinating lives, observers can see Harlem's many historic districts and cultural landmarks. From its housing stock of beautiful brownstones to its stunning architectural buildings and churches, Harlem's history lives through its array of buildings and structures, some dating back to the late nineteenth century.

In addition to the numerous individual landmarks, there are "historic districts" throughout Harlem. These districts mark the places where architects such as Richard S. Rosenstock, Frederick P. Dinkelberg and Henri Fouchaux built some of the most stylish and detailed homes of the late nineteenth and early twentieth centuries. The first black architect registered in New York State, Vertner Tandy, designed the last building constructed in the Hamilton Heights Historic District and Extension in 1948—the Ivey Delph Apartments at 19 Hamilton Terrace.[16] The Hamilton Heights Historic District, named after the first U.S. Treasury secretary, Alexander Hamilton, includes the Sugar Hill section of Harlem and is separated by the northeast and northwest sections of the community. Architect Tandy also designed the estate for the first African American female millionaire, Madame C.J. Walker. Her estate, the Villa Lewaro, was built in Irvington-on-Hudson, New York. Together with fellow architect George W. Foster Jr., Tandy also designed Harlem's Saint Philip's Episcopal Church, the home of New York's oldest African American Episcopal church congregation.

With so much history in Harlem, it seems fitting that the nation's premier facility for archiving and researching African American culture would be located in Harlem. The Schomburg Center for Research in Black Culture, located at 135th Street and Lenox Avenue, is renowned for its collections and artifacts on black history. The library is part of the New York Public Library system and is one of several Harlem public libraries that have been designated landmarks. Schomburg was originally known as the 135th Street branch. However, during the 1920s, a perceptive branch librarian took note of the many changes taking place in Harlem and on her own started a small library of black history within the library. In 1925, the branch was renamed the 135th Street Branch Division of Negro Literature. In 1926, the library acquired the massive collection of African history from bibliophile Arturo Alphonso Schomburg, who was born in Puerto Rico to a black mother and German father. The library was renamed in his honor in 1972 and in 1982 was designated a historic landmark.

The renowned Schomburg Center for Research in Black Culture has been documenting the lives of people of African descent for more than eighty years.

One of Harlem's historic public libraries.

HISTORIC DISTRICTS

There are at least seven official historic districts within Harlem and numerous architectural and historic landmarks. These landmarks include the former homes of history-making politicians, writers, artists and musicians; police stations and firehouses; colleges and hospitals; an armory; theaters; and a number of historic churches. In addition, still standing in Harlem are some of the last remaining nineteenth-century brick homes with wooden porches, which were common during those years. This includes Astor Row on West 130th Street, a block of twenty-eight homes with double wooden doors and porches, with some built in pairs while the other homes were attached at the rear. Most of these houses have been rehabilitated and restored through preservation efforts, but as these remnants of Harlem's early history are preserved, a new Harlem is being developed just a few feet away. Signs advertising new condominium developments hang on newly developed buildings just around

A Harlem apartment building billboard promoting a cable television show based in Harlem.

the corner. Still, just as the Astor Row homes remain, throughout Harlem markers of history can be seen nearly everywhere you turn.

Audubon Terrace Historic District

Located near 155th Street and Broadway, Audubon Terrace is on the edge between Harlem and Washington Heights. Designated a historic district in 1979, Audubon Terrace is considered "one of America's first planned cultural centers." It was established on the estate of John James Audubon, an artist and naturalist. The center's complex was conceived by a Spanish scholar, philanthropist and heir to the Southern Pacific Railroad fortune, Archer M. Huntington.

In 1904, Huntington founded the Hispanic Society of America. With the help of both his wife and his cousin, Huntington led the development of cultural facilities at the site. He eventually commissioned his cousin Charles

Harlem History Since 1900

P. Huntington to design a gallery and a library for the center. From 1907 through 1912, several other cultural organizations were located at the site, including the American Geographical Society and the Museum of the American Indian.

Saint Nicholas Historic District

The Saint Nicholas Historic District was designated a historic district in 1967. This area between Frederick Douglass Boulevard and Lenox Avenue includes a four-block area conceived by developer David H. King Jr., who had worked on a number of New York City projects previously. He knew many of the city's leading architects of the time and sought them out for this project. King led the project, which included the development of 146 row houses and three apartment buildings.

Most of the homes were on West 138th and West 139th Streets, an area that would become known as Striver's Row, referring to the aspirations of many of the black residents who eventually moved to the area. Many of the affluent professionals and artists of the day lived in the area, including singer and songwriter Eubie Blake, who lived at 236 West 138th Street; bandleader

The corner of 116th Street and Frederick Douglass Boulevard, where subway station trains are heading "uptown."

Acclaimed jazz composer and pianist James Hubert "Eubie" Blake played in a Harlem-based orchestra early in his music career.

Fletcher Henderson at 228 West 139th Street; musician W.C. Handy at 232 West 139th Street; boxer Harry Wills at 245 West 139th Street; and architect Vertner Tandy at 221 West 139th Street. Many other famous people of the era also resided in the Striver's Row area.

Three architectural firms designed the homes that made up the community. James Brown Lord designed the red brick and brownstone Georgian-inspired rows on the south side of West 138th Street; Bruce Price was responsible for the yellow brick Colonial Revival houses with white limestone and terra cotta trim on the north side of West 138th Street and the south side of West 139th Street; and McKim, Mead & White partner Stanford White designed the elegant Italian Renaissance–inspired row in dark mottled brick with brownstone and terra cotta trim on the north side of West 139th Street.[17]

Mount Morris Park Historic District

The Mount Morris Park Historic District began its development in the late nineteenth century and was closely linked to what was then known as Mount Morris Park. Mount Morris Park, located along Fifth Avenue, was renamed Marcus Garvey Park in 1973 in honor of one of the first well-known black nationalists, Marcus Garvey, a native of Jamaica who once lived in Harlem. In 1971, Mount Morris Park was named a historic district. In the late nineteenth and early twentieth centuries, affluent Protestant and German Jews started developing the community largely built around tree-lined Lenox Avenue. Most of the homes built in the area at the time were in the neo-Renaissance, neo-Grec and Romanesque Revival styles.

Many of the buildings that were built were churches of varying faiths, including Episcopalian, Unitarian and Presbyterian, as well as several synagogues. However, in the 1920s, as Harlem's population changed and more Caribbeans and African Americans moved to the area, many of these religious institutions were converted to houses of worship for different faiths to accommodate Harlem's new residents.

Hamilton Heights Historic Districts

Harlem's Hamilton Heights neighborhood includes four separate historic districts that comprise some of Harlem's most notable communities. Named after Alexander Hamilton, development of the area began in the 1880s around the same time that an elevated rail line was built, making it easy to travel to lower Manhattan. Located in upper Harlem, the historic districts include areas north of City College along Convent and St. Nicholas Avenues. Known for the stunning architecture of its homes, buildings and churches, the area is equally as culturally rich, with many famous artists and musicians having lived in the area. Sugar Hill, a well-known neighborhood where many affluent African Americans lived during the 1920s, including Ralph Ellison, Adam Clayton Powell Jr. and Duke Ellington, is located in this part of Harlem.

INDIVIDUAL LANDMARKS

Harlem, New York, is rich in history and full of numerous historic landmarks. Wherever you are in Harlem, you are likely close to one of these landmarks. Individual landmarks in Harlem are plentiful and include Columbia University and its recognizable columned main library, Low Memorial Library; Riverside Church, the Alexander Hamilton House; City College; the former Regent Theatre, which is now First Corinthian Baptist Church; Hotel Theresa; New York Public Library's Schomburg Center for Research in Black Culture; Mother African Methodist Episcopal Zion Church; Abyssinian Baptist Church; Community House; and many, many more. Harlem consists of several neighborhoods—Morningside Heights, Hamilton Heights, Central Harlem and East and West Harlem—each with its own vibrant history and landmarks. Many of the buildings and churches in these neighborhoods feature Romanesque Revival and neoclassical architectural elements, as well as Queen Anne–style structures.

> ## Harlem Sites Among 11 Called Landmarks
>
> The Landmarks Preservation Commission announced today the designation of eleven new Landmarks, including the Metropolitan Museum of Art, Carnegie Hall, Grand Central Terminal and Hamilton Grange.
> Geoffrey Platt, chairman of the Commission, also announced the designation of the Seventh Regiment Armory, 643 Park Avenue; Saint George's Church, 16th Street and Stuyvesant Square; the Dyckman House, Broadway at 204th Street; and the Morris-Jumel Mansion, 160th Street and Edgecombe Avenue.
> The Commission also designated the 115th Street Branch of the New York Public Library, located at 203 W. 115th St.; the Watch Tower in Mount Morris Park opposite 122nd Street; and the Water Tower in Highbridge Park at 173rd Street.
>
> #### Country Home
> Hamilton Grange, located at 287 Convent Avenue, was Alexander Hamilton's country home during the last years of his life. The Commission said "As the building is now situated, the Grange cannot be made to reflect either its architect's conception or its condition when it was Alexander Hamilton's residence.
> "However, Congress has passed legislation establishing the Grange as a national memorial and appropriating funds for its restoration contingent on the satisfaction of the Secretary of the Department of the Interior that 'the lands which have been donated are sufficient to assure the relocation of the Grange ...'"
> "Henry G. Schmidt, Superintendent of the New York City National Park Service Group, which has the responsibility for carrying out the Federal legislation, comments 'We are pleased to be able to open the Grange to the public at this time even though temporarily it must be on a reduced scale, but we find that the fabric and structure of the building are in good shape, and it is our hope that a suitable site can soon be acquired in the immediate neighborhood, and restoration — for which we have complete plans — proceed promptly.'"
>
> #### Alternate Sites
> The Landmarks Commission added "The National Park Service is preparing several alternate site proposals, all within one or two blocks of the present site, and there have been recent meetings involving the Local Planning Board and other interested people in the neighborhood, the National Park Service, and this Commission. We note here with satisfaction that there is every indication that a good new site will indeed soon be agreed upon."
> The Mount Morris Park Watch Tower is the last remaining fire lookout tower of its type in the City. Fire watch towers were used in the City until 1878.
> The Morris-Jumel Mansion, a handsome 1765 Georgian house, was lived in at one time by Aaron Burr. The Dyckman House is a restoration of a typical Dutch Colonial farmhouse.
> The Commission's designations are subject to review within ninety days by the Board of Estimate. The Landmarks Commission will review any changes proposed for buildings it designates as Landmarks. The law gives the Commission the responsibility of working with owners to preserve designated New York City Landmarks.

Several Harlem structures were named landmarks in 1967, including a New York Public Library branch on West 115th Street and the watchtower in what is now Marcus Garvey Park.

Romanesque Revival buildings—many of them churches—were built between the 1850s and 1900 and feature rounded arches on doorways and windows and belt courses—continuous rows of stones, tiles or bricks—in structure walls. Additional Harlem landmarks include:

The Croton Aqueduct's two gatehouses, one at 432-24 West 119th and the other at 135th Street, were built to control the fresh water flow in New York City. The 135th Street gatehouse, the oldest of the two, is constructed with granite and brownstone and was designated a landmark in 1981. Its counterpart at 119th Street remained in operation until 1990 and was designated a landmark in 2000.

A number of apartment buildings, including the Graham Court Apartments and Washington Apartments in the 1900 and 2000 blocks of Adam Clayton Powell Boulevard and the Dunbar Apartments and Harlem River Houses, have been named landmarks. The Dunbar Apartments, located along 149th Street to 150th between Frederick Douglass and Adam Clayton Powell Jr. Boulevard, was like many other Harlem properties and was home to prominent figures such as A. Philip Randolph and W.E.B. Du Bois.

Many other landmarks stand throughout Harlem, including the Union Theological Seminary, numerous churches, several police and fire stations, the Hamilton Grange National Monument at 287 Convent Avenue, several

Arturo Alphonso Schomburg was an avid collector of African history who once loaned items to the 135th Street branch of the New York Public Library. Today, that branch bears his name.

New York Public Library branches and several theaters, including the former Regent Theater, one of the first fancy movie theaters in America; it is now First Corinthian Baptist Church. The Hamilton Theater at 146th and Broadway was a former vaudeville house that in the late 1920s was one of the first movie theaters in New York to show "talking pictures."

Historic Harlem Jazz Stoop

A famous photograph of fifty-seven jazz greats was taken on a stoop in Harlem by Art Kane of *Esquire* magazine. The picture was featured in the 1995 documentary *A Great Day in Harlem*. The musicians gathered in front of the house located at 17 East 126th Street between Fifth and Madison Avenues. A producer and writer for the documentary, Jean Bach, says the house was chosen mainly because of its proximity to the 125th Street train station. At one time, the house was decrepit and in poor shape, but it has recently been painted and renovated. The house still stands today.[18]

409 Edgecombe Avenue

For many well-known artists, writers, political activists and jazz greats of early to mid-twentieth-century Harlem, it was the neighborhood they worked in and the community they belonged to. Many of them called Harlem home and lived in two prestigious properties on Edgecombe Avenue. From the 1930s through the 1950s, 409 Edgecombe Avenue was the most prestigious address in New York City for African Americans. The twelve-story building was originally called Colonial Parkway Apartments and was built on a ridge overlooking central Harlem. Some notable people who once lived at 409 Edgecombe Avenue include painter Aaron Douglas; bandleader Jimmie Lunceford; Julius C. Bledsoe, a singer and actor known for singing "Ole Man River"; black physician May Edward Chinn; scholar, activist and founder of the NAACP W.E.B. Du Bois; NAACP executives Walter White and Roy Wilkins; and Thurgood Marshall, who became the first African American Supreme Court justice.

555 Edgecombe Avenue

Another prestigious address in Harlem was 555 Edgecombe Avenue. Originally known as the Roger Morris, the building was constructed in 1916. At that time, apartments in the building were only leased to white tenants. However, as the Harlem community was changing, in 1939–40, the tenants of 555 Edgecombe Avenue became exclusively African American. Some well-known tenants include actor and producer Canada Lee, singer and actor Paul Robeson and jazz great Count Basie.

THE PEOPLE OF HARLEM

There is a saying that goes something like this: "A church building alone does not make a church. What makes a church is its people." If one were talking about the "church of Harlem," this church would have a spectacular congregation.

Throughout the twentieth century, the people of Harlem have made the community the extraordinary place that it is. There is an energy that flows through Harlem that is infectious. Prior to and during the Harlem Renaissance in the 1920s and 1930s, African Americans were drawn to the area. Many journeyed to Harlem seeking better work opportunities than the South provided. Others, such as musicians and other creative types, were lured by both the opportunities to work and the creative energy. Black professionals—doctors, lawyers and teachers—were also drawn to Harlem and helped establish it as a place to be for progressive people.

It is interesting to see how Harlem today resembles Harlem of yesteryear in so many ways. Redevelopment of properties, new business influx, a new arts renaissance and changing demographics; these are the same things that were taking place in Harlem more than one hundred years ago at the beginning of the twentieth century.

Before Harlem became a predominantly African American community, both Jews and Italians lived in the area. Near the less attractive areas of Harlem, on the periphery of the middle-class community, lived people bypassed by Harlem's late nineteenth-century affluence. Italian immigrants crowded in "common tenements" from 110th to 125th Streets, east of Third Avenue to the river. In the 1890s, the poverty of "Harlem's Little Italy" seemed a glaring incongruity in a neighborhood known as the home of the "great middle-class population, the very cream of our citizenship."[19]

From the 1880s through 1910, Italians settled in the area east of Third Avenue to the river, closely followed by Eastern Europeans. The newcomers settled down and flourished. In the 1930s, the Italian community in Harlem was the largest in the country.[20]

East Harlem's boundaries are from East 96th Street to East 142nd Street, Fifth Avenue to the East River. Because its internal boundaries are ever-changing as people move into and migrate within the neighborhood, East Harlem is many places at once—El Barrio, Italian Harlem, the East Harlem Triangle, the West Indian Village, Little Mexico and scattered enclaves of Africans. Today's ethnic mix and "inner neighborhoods" continue a long history of diversity. For more than three hundred years, a constant progression of working-class immigrants has shaped the cultural landscape of East Harlem.[21]

For Yvette Seda, who grew up visiting family who still lives in East Harlem, the changing demographics is one of the big differences she has noticed since coming to East Harlem as a kid.

> *The only difference now is the whole different culture. A lot of different cultures, a lot of different languages. That's different. A lot more people. 'Cause when I was growing up, it was just mainly all Puerto Ricans then, that's what I know, mainly all Puerto Ricans. But now, it's very different now.*
>
> *What I really miss in New York is that conga beat. When I was a young girl, everybody, especially the girls, was playing congas.*

Seda, who has lived in the Philadelphia area for nearly twenty years, speaks fondly of New York, and it's obvious she could easily return. "I like the people 'cause it's always fun, you know. I miss New York. I miss the people. I miss everything in New York really."

Seda left New York for Philadelphia to assist her mother, who had decided to move to Philly.

> *Every time I stop in New York, if nobody wants to go with me, I hop on the train and walk myself. I go myself. There is something to do there by yourself. You don't even need friends to hang out in New York.* [laughter] *And one thing about New York, East Harlem, whatever, you don't need to go outside. You can just open the window and take over the view. You can just go to the window and go to the fire escape. That's what I do. I go to*

the fire escape. I sit there and I see everything. Everything. The people. The fights. Everything. Just to sit on the fire escape. I will eat there. There's so much to do in New York. You don't have to go watch TV. You can just open the window, go to the fire escape and you see. Beautiful.

In East Harlem, Seda says much of what's new in the area is the people. Around 116th and Lexington, she says, is primarily Mexican now—"Little Mexico." In fact, a number of Mexican restaurants have opened near 116th and Third Avenue and 102nd and 103rd Streets and Lexington. Bodegas in East Harlem, according to Seda, were all Puerto Rican owned. Now, she says, many are Dominican or Mexican owned.

The Residents and the Community

One thing that is immediately noticeable when speaking to somebody from Harlem is their confidence and their sense of pride. Ask them about Harlem and their eyes light up. Their body shifts positions, and they are eager to speak. When describing Harlem, it has been said that "Harlem is love." And that is what you sense when you talk to Harlem's own, no matter if they are talking about Harlem's glory days or some of Harlem's past dark nights.

"I lived in Harlem for ten years, and I like Harlem. I'm not moving out of Harlem. And I feel a lot of changes in Harlem," says Lora Bell, a forty-something maintenance worker. Accompanied by her husband and four-year-old grandson, Caleb, she talks about life in Harlem and the future of the community.

"What's taking place in Harlem right now is real estate and co-ops," she says. What Bell is referring to is the exponential increase in the development and redevelopment of Harlem properties. Everywhere you look, either something is being worked on or something new is being built.

"I grew up in Harlem my whole life, and it's changed," says Leslie Forster, twenty-three, who is also a maintenance worker.

It's changed now. Mostly everything is more commercial compared to how it used to be. On 125th, everybody used to come out and just sell things, but now you need licenses for most of the selling. It's hard to come about getting those licenses for a lot of vendors, so I mean, you still see people selling CDs and movies and all that compared to how people used to sell African paintings, statues, incense and fragrances. You don't see any of that anymore, so that's how it's changed a lot. It used to be…I guess it was

Meetings slated on Harlem brownstones sale

By SIMON ANEKWE

The City Administration will sell some 235 of its Harlem brownstones next year, with 65 percent of the total reserved for Harlem residents only and the other 35 percent open to residents and non-residents of that Black community.

Community Board 10 which covers Central Harlem, has set Nov. 16 as the date for its ULURP public hearing on 118 of the brownstones which lie within its domain. The meeting will be held at the Adam Clayton Powell Jr. State Office Building, 163 West 125th St., starting at 6 p.m. in the second floor Art Gallery.

The housing committee of Community Board Nine, which has the other 117 brownstones, is expected to set a date for a similar public hearing when it meets, Nov. 14. This West Harlem area is bounded by 110th St., Morningside and St. Nicholas Parks to 155th St., over to the Hudson River.

The Board 10 area borders the Board Nine boundary in the west, with Central Park North, Fifth Ave. and 155th St. as other boundaries. Community Board 11, in East Harlem, is developing its own plans for brownstone sales; and Board 12 covering Washington Heights did not participate in the talks with the City Housing Preservation and Development Dept. Board 12 has only a few such buildings within its area.

Talks on the brownstone sale have been going on for over a year. HPD Deputy Commissioner Robert Davis said the city has taken care to eliminate any cause to fear gentrification, by not supporting any program that would change the "character of Harlem."

City Councilman Fred Samuel has been a focal point of the negotiations market rate, for part of the cost.

This would cover the 25 percent of the cost that purchasers have to put down. They would get the J 51 tax abatement now prevailing. HUDC would give purchasers technical advice especially in preparation for the sale by sealed bids.

Last minute hitches delayed release of the buildings in Board Nine. Those in Board 10 are numbers: 212 W. 112th St., 225, 227, 231, 259 W. 113th; 320 W. 115th, 102, 109, 358 W. 118th St., 158 W. 119th St.; 24, 34, 38, 70, 102, 119, 129, 131, 152, 229, 231, 241, 351, 353, 367, 369 W. 129th; 16, 18, 157, 159, 254, 341, 350, 352 W. 121st St.

Also: 113, 149, 159, 213, 214, 218, 231, 233, 241, 251, 353, 357 West 122nd; 2, 132, 152, 208, 210, 232, 234, 236, 238, 247, 260 W. 123rd St.; 119, 149 and 171 W. 126th St.; 403, 525, 531, 533, 543, 549 Manhattan Ave.; 185, 208, 243, 245, 253, 449 Lenox Ave.; 2066, 2072, 2074, 2086 Fifth Ave.; 4, 16, 18, 28, 35, 102, 106, 115, 124 W. 130th St.; 205 W. 131st St.

Also, 103, 105, 119, 125, 131, 150, 146, 150, 222, 266 W. 132nd St.; 120, 148, 162 W. 133rd St.; 253 W. 134th St.; 113, 115, 117, 120, 123, 131, 143, 145, 161, 213, 249, 256, 313 W. 136th St.; 245 W. 137th St.; 203, 316 W. 138th St. and 214 W. 1139th St.; the last three in the famed Striver's Row.

HUDC and Rep. Rangel's office have been working on Washington for federal funds, possibly UDAG, to bring the prices down to levels that a person on a $20,000 annual income can afford. However two or three members of a family can join to purchase a building, with each owning one floor.

Mr. Samuel also said that the HUDC board of directors would ask the State for funding to help make the buildings affordable for the mid-income Harlemite, even though others on higher incomes will need such help.

Carver and Freedom National Banks as well as United Mutual Life Insurance, Harlem's three financial institutions, have been asked to see how they can participate in the financing, at below market rates of interest, the Councilman said. Meetings have also been set up with outside financial institutions, he added.

Commissioner Davis said the city is targeting the brownstone sale for April 1985, by which time the financing arrangements should have been completed.

Above: When Harlem deteriorated in the 1970s and 1980s, the city took over a number of brownstones and then offered them for sale at low prices. This article is about meetings being held on the sale of these homes.

Left: Street vendors have always been part of Harlem culture, especially on 125th Street. When Mayor Rudolph Giuliani was in office, tensions were high as Giuliani moved to oust vendors.

The People of Harlem

more fun because it was a different mayor. This was around the time when Mayor [David] *Dinkins was in charge when I was coming up.*

Although much is changing physically in Harlem, some core ideas and values have remained the same. "Harlem has so much history, " says Forster, "plus it's residential everywhere in Harlem. And there are so many buildings you can just go to different communities and you got family everywhere. Back in the early days with Harlem—not early days, but you know, '70s and '80s—it was mainly a black community."

Today, while Harlem is still predominantly African American and Spanish, the economic and developmental changes taking place throughout the neighborhood are attracting people from all cultures.

"I'd say it's real diverse. It's real diverse. You got everything in Harlem," says Forster. "Spanish to black to even now, this new age, you see a lot of Asians. I got Asian people in my building now," he says.

In fact, according to the 2010 census, the Asian population in Harlem and East Harlem has grown more than 200 percent.[22] Many of these Chinese

Along with numerous restaurants in Harlem, food vendors offering everything from fresh fruit to water ice can be seen throughout Harlem during hot summer days.

residents say the reason for the increase is a "good environment" but mainly bigger apartments and cheaper rents.

Yvette Seda came to New York with her father from Puerto Rico when she was a young girl. Although she now lives in nearby Philadelphia, she is excited when talking about her experience growing up in the Bronx and East Harlem.

"I was raised in the Bronx. Made in the Bronx really. Made in the Bronx. Born in Puerto Rico. I came to the Bronx when I was forty days old. I lived in the Bronx. My father died when I was five and my brother was six. Then we moved back to Puerto Rico. But when I was like nine years old, we came back to the Bronx," says Seda.

Seda, who grew up in the Bronx but spent a lot of time with family in East Harlem as a kid, says the area is changing nowadays. When she was growing up, she says East Harlem was "mainly all Puerto Ricans."

"Puerto Ricans are the majority [of Latinos] in New York, but now we have lots of other cultures, which is beautiful." Now, she says, Haitians, Jamaicans, Africans and other Latinos such as Mexicans and Dominicans are living and working in the area.

Although Seda, who has two adult sons, lives in Philadelphia, she tries to visit East Harlem as often as she can. And she says she has also noticed a change in business ownership when traveling to East Harlem.

"What I see is a lot of different cultures has lots of business now. You go to El Barrio now when you go to the stores, Haitians owns it or Jamaicans. And what's the difference from way back was mainly the business was like Jewish. Mainly they were all businesspeople. Now it's different cultures. Now they have more business," Seda says.

One thing that has appeared to have stayed the same in Harlem is the people and their sense of style. At least a small part of this can be attributed to different decades and different eras. For instance, look at any old photograph from the early twentieth century through the mid-twentieth century. Everyone pictured will be well dressed—men in suits, dress pants and collared shirts, women in dresses, skirts and hats. This is different from the current age of "casual days" and "dress-down Fridays." In earlier days, everyone was dressed up every day, all day, partially because that was the way it was. Sneakers and jeans were not yet part of the attire because they had not yet become part of the culture.

In Harlem, just a glance along sections of 125th Street in 1956 and the retail shops alone gives one a glimpse of the fashion sense of the neighborhood people. For instance, sandwiched between the former Harlem Opera House

The People of Harlem

A look at Harlem's 125th Street in earlier days, 1949.

and the renowned Apollo Theatre, there was a men's store, hat shop, pants shop and wine store. Even advertisements in local newspapers such as the *New York Amsterdam News* reflected the tastes of "Harlemites."

In a 1935 newspaper ad, one Midtown fur coat retailer, who was appealing to the entertainment world that was so much a part of Harlem at the time, even used the word "Movieland" in its company name. In a large ad that was at least a third of the page, they advertised Silver Fox, Jap Mink and Persian Lamb furs, among many others. And they invited buyers to visit their "seven floors of furs."

Styles change and new eras begin, however, and in Harlem, that sense of style remains. Style is more than just how people dress; it is about how they carry themselves.

"I just think that's Harlem, period. Harlem always has got the swag, that confidence," says Forster, using the term "swag" that many young people use to reference a person's style or demeanor. "So no matter where, you stand out, I feel. You can be anywhere, across town, uptown, downtown, you can still tell a Harlem person," Les Forster says. "His whole swag, his aura, everything. How he stands, how he wears his clothes, how he looks. Just that extra confidence knowing you about something, something important.

I think that's with all Harlem people though. That stands out from all five boroughs. Harlem's got that look, that swag. That's been there since the '40s, when people used to do it in a tux and all that."

Nowadays in Harlem, people in the community still like to look good, but it is a different time in society. As suits, wingtips and fedoras ruled in earlier days, today's culture is hip-hop fashionable. For the younger crowd, baggy jeans and big T-shirts or jeans and button-down dress shirts dominate. And sneakers, lots and lots of sneakers.

For women, jeans are still a staple, along with short skirts and big heels. Four-inch heels have returned with both a stiletto-style heel and a fat, chunky heel. For the older crowd, men will suit up, of course; however, now if the suit is for a social event, some jacket cuts may be longer, and they will often be designed in less traditional styles and in a variety of colors for younger men. For older women in Harlem, individual women have their own styles, but one thing that has stayed the same over the years is the hat—church ladies and their hats. Visit Harlem on any Sunday morning and you will see women with hats in all different shapes and sizes. Wearing a hat to church has been a tradition among African American women for decades.

When you talk to Harlemites, it becomes clear that change has been coming to Harlem for a long time, especially when you start talking about businesses—which ones used to be in the area, which ones remain and the future of business in the community.

Natalie, a thirty-something who was born and raised in Harlem, lived on 112th Street. She echoes what some in Harlem believe, and that is that Harlem is changing, yes, and with this change there is a sense of loss in the community. "I feel it's missing its culture, its heart," she says.

Natalie has memories of an old Woolworth's store on 125th Street that she and her mom would visit to shop and have lunch. She remembers shoe shops and other stores that are now gone, but it is what they did when they were there that made the stores themselves and her experience in them memorable.

"Most businesses would make it a little different to let you know that you're in Harlem. That's what made things special." Nowadays, she says, businesses in general are more sterile and generic. No artwork. No décor. No mention of Harlem's history. She even recalls a favorite dry cleaner that was located on Lenox Avenue between 111th and 112th Streets. The cleaners was owned by an Asian couple who had "been there forever," says Natalie. So connected to the shop, she still continued to go there even after she moved away from the neighborhood. She says she found out the cleaners was gone just by chance when she was going to the shop to do business. "I was shocked," she says. "They'd been there forever, and they're gone. Why?"

Darren Jameson, a forty-nine-year-old divorced father of one son, has been a lifelong resident of Harlem. He notices the changes going on in Harlem and feels that African Americans are going to get "pushed out of here" due to all of the development in Harlem. He says that at the corner of 125th and Lenox, an empty fenced-in lot will eventually be turned into some sort of luxury building. And, he says, this is just one of many.

An intelligent, clean-cut man with a low Caesar haircut and no facial hair, Jameson grew up on the east side of Harlem and knows all too well the ups and downs of life in Harlem. Years ago, he spent five years in prison for drugs. He says that today you still see the devastating affect that the influx of drugs has had on the Harlem community.

Historians and History Makers

When thinking of Harlem, it is understandable that one thinks primarily of the area's history of art and culture. The Harlem Renaissance usually tops the list of what people know about the community. But aside from the arts, a number of acclaimed individuals who have lived or worked in Harlem have been extremely influential in American history and African American history in particular.

W.E.B. Du Bois. Paul Robeson. Marcus Garvey. Madame C.J. Walker. A. Philip Randolph. Thurgood Marshall. Adam Clayton Powell Jr. The list goes on.

Numerous icons of the civil rights era have lived and toiled here. And virtually all of the jazz masters—Duke Ellington, Ella Fitzgerald, Charlie Parker, Dizzy Gillespie, Billie Holiday, Charlie Mingus—and many others have been part of Harlem's eclectic community.

All of these men and women, who have each individually left an indelible mark on American history, lived, thrived and socialized in Harlem. Although much has been said about the entertainment and nightclub culture that once encapsulated Harlem in the twentieth century, the people of Harlem have always been social and socially conscious.

Perhaps no area in the community was as thriving with political activity as the corner of 125th Street and Seventh Avenue. This intersection could quite possibly be the most historic corner in all of America. Presidents

NYPD officers walk among Harlem residents and visitors along 125th Street near franchise stores that line the street. The African American flag flies in the background.

and presidential candidates have spoken here. African American political activists of all stripes have bellowed here. It was a tradition years ago for people to congregate here, stand on a soapbox and shout—with a bullhorn or without—about whatever political issue of the day they saw fit. Remnants of this activity can still be found today.

In addition to presenting and offering knowledge, one could also go to this area to receive knowledge. A known treasure in the community because of its wealth of information was the African Memorial National Bookstore. Owners Willis Huggins and Lewis Micheaux were left-wing ideologues, and their voluminous stock reflected their philosophy.[23] Du Bois, Robeson, Randolph and Marshall, all well educated and learned men, were customers of the store. The bookstore, which was located across the street from the legendary Hotel Theresa, closed in the mid-1960s as new business development set in.

Today in Harlem, there are several independent bookstores featuring books written by and about Africans and African Americans. Hue-Man Bookstore & Café, located at 2319 Frederick Douglass Boulevard,[24] has been a mainstay in the Harlem community for years. And just as the former African Memorial National Bookstore served as an unofficial gathering place

The People of Harlem

and meeting ground for intellectuals and social activists, Hue-Man serves a similar crowd today. Many well-known national and international authors hold signings there. Inside the store, one can often overhear conversations on the issues of the day.

A little farther uptown, Sisters Uptown Bookstore at 1942 Amsterdam Avenue offers a similar variety of books and, in addition, hosts a number of author appearances and other cultural events and programs. Smaller than Hue-Man, Sisters Uptown is relished in the community. It is not surprising that a bookstore in Harlem would attract leaders of the African-American community.

The Renaissance period is well known and documented with the multitudes of creative works that were produced; however, what is not often talked about is Harlem's role in jumpstarting a number of African American journalism products that were born in the area. Numerous media outlets, including radio shows, newspapers and magazines, began in Harlem. Many of them were in some way connected to the most famous building in Harlem—the Hotel Theresa.

John Johnson, the late publishing mogul who started *Jet* and *Ebony* magazines, was just one of many media professionals with ties to the Hotel Theresa. Virtually all of the New York newspapers that covered African American life operated in some capacity out of the Hotel Theresa. The *New York Amsterdam News*. The *New York Age*. The *Pittsburgh Courier*. Each of these papers had representatives working out of the Hotel Theresa.

The historic former Hotel Theresa, which was the center of black Harlem life in the mid-twentieth century.

Entrance to the *New York Amsterdam News*'s offices on Eighth Avenue. The newspaper has operated out of the same building for decades.

During the Harlem Renaissance, the creative spirits of those such as Jean Toomer, Zora Neale Hurston, Countee Cullen, Langston Hughes, Aaron Douglas, Alain Locke, James Van Der Zee and others gathered at the Hotel Theresa, mingling with various entertainment, sports and political figures.

The Hotel Theresa was located on the southwest corner of Seventh Avenue and 125th Street. Called the Great Black Way, Seventh Avenue has always been Harlem's most beautiful boulevard. This two-way artery, sectioned for uptown and downtown traffic, was divided by a narrow strip of beautiful trees and manicured grass and gardens. It was Harlem's principal business boulevard. Seventh Avenue mirrored Harlem's life.[25]

One newspaper that was very influential in reporting about the comings and goings of celebrities and non-celebrities in Harlem was not based in New York State but instead in Pennsylvania. The *Pittsburgh Courier* was the premier journal that people inside and outside of Harlem looked to in order to find the latest entertainment happenings. It was not until 1940 that the Hotel Theresa opened its doors to blacks, and that's when a columnist named Billy Rowe stepped up to take his place as a legendary recorder of Harlem's entertainment history by writing about all of the happenings at the famous Hotel Theresa. Rowe obtained a huge following of people in New York City and beyond. As Rowe became Harlem's leading entertainment reporter, there was another *Pittsburgh Courier* reporter who was leaving her mark.

Evelyn Cunningham was a pioneering woman who had a distinguished career in journalism before becoming a champion for women's rights and holding positions in the office of a former New York mayor, Governor Nelson Rockefeller and President Richard Nixon. As a reporter with the *Pittsburgh Courier*, she covered many of the country's most tumultuous events—lynchings across the South in the 1940s and '50s and, during the '60s, the civil rights movement. From 1961 to 1966, she hosted her own radio show on WLIB-AM. A longtime resident of Harlem, Cunningham once worked as an assistant to baseball legend Jackie Robinson, who at one time had businesses in Harlem. Evelyn Cunningham died in April 2010 in New York City at the age of ninety-four.

Rowe and Cunningham worked for the *Pittsburgh Courier* when the newspaper had offices throughout the northeast region, including Harlem. The newspaper's offices were directly

An advertisement in a 1940 edition of the *Pittsburgh Courier* advertises the Hotel Theresa. During those years, the newspaper covered the happenings in Harlem very closely.

across the street from the Hotel Theresa, giving its writers a prime view of hotel events. But the *Pittsburgh Courier* is just one of several newspapers that were thoroughly reporting on the Harlem area. The *New York Age* and the *Amsterdam News*, which still publishes weekly, were both diligently covering the Harlem community. And these publications were the forerunner to several other publications, both local and national, that would emerge out of Harlem. One company that began in Harlem became a renowned publisher of magazines addressing the African American community.

In the early 1940s, a young man from Arkansas named John H. Johnson spent a number of months in the Hotel Theresa talking about starting a new magazine. He envisioned a pocket-size publication that would condense newspaper and magazine stories about black life. This idea turned out to be *Negro Digest*, which he began publishing in 1943. Two years later, Johnson started *Ebony*, and it was followed by *Jet* in 1951. The magazines published by the Johnson Publishing Company added even more luster to the already famous Hotel Theresa.[26]

On August 8, 2005, John Harold Johnson, commonly known throughout his life as "John H. Johnson, publisher," died at the age of eighty-seven. With his dream of creating publications for African American people fulfilled, John Johnson's publishing company today is based in Chicago, Illinois, where it has had offices for many years. Today, the company is run by his daughter and other family members. Both *Ebony* and *Jet* are considered trailblazing publications for African Americans, and both magazines are published to this day. They are among the first national magazines in the United States to intimately cover the lives of African Americans and the issues that affect them. Over the years, the company expanded into fashion, cosmetics and book publishing.

But the introduction of Johnson's publications was just the beginning of numerous media that would emerge. Several publications would be started through national political organizations that would establish offices in Harlem. Both the NAACP and the Urban League established offices in Harlem and often operated out of the Hotel Theresa.

Crisis, which was started by the NAACP and edited by W.E.B. Du Bois, was one of a number of publications that would arise to address the political issues facing African Americans. *Messenger* magazine preceded *Ebony* and *Jet* and was started in 1917 by A. Philip Randolph and Chandler Owen.

The elegant Hotel Theresa was the meeting place for black celebrities and black notables. It was home to the Skyline Ballroom, which hosted some of Harlem's ritziest events. The hotel's history within the entertainment world

The People of Harlem

A. Philip Randolph was a labor leader and activist who worked tirelessly for the rights of African American workers.

alone is fascinating. But along with being a center for celebrity gatherings, the hotel also became known as a crucial pit stop for anyone participating in the world of politics. If you had something to say and you wanted the people of Harlem and beyond to hear it, then a stop at the Hotel Theresa was practically mandatory. Both international and U.S. presidents, as well as high-profile political activists, have made the Hotel Theresa a destination.

It is interesting that the Hotel Theresa got its start as an entertainment gathering place, but in the '50s and '60s, as the political climate changed, so, too, did the events surrounding the hotel. This also shows just how much the hotel was part of the community. Already accustomed to celebrities on site, during this time, the patrons changed from entertainment personalities to political movers and shakers. The hotel still hosted celebrities, of course; nevertheless, the times were changing.

Political leaders of different stripes made their way to 125th Street and Seventh Avenue. In the late '50s, the first president of an independent Ghana, Dr. Kwame Nkrumah, visited the hotel. Cuba's Fidel Castro made a famous

The former Hotel Theresa in Harlem, now known as the Theresa Tower, was the playground for the black entertainment elite. The building underwent renovations in 2010.

visit to the hotel in 1960. Former U.S. president John F. Kennedy also visited the hotel in 1960. Soviet premier Nikita Kruschev and a host of other high-ranking world leaders would make their way to Harlem and the Hotel Theresa.

Harlem "Firsts"

So much was happening concurrently in Harlem during the first half of the twentieth century that it is understandable for someone reviewing these years to get absorbed by the events of one aspect of life and barely even notice the others. The Great Migration of blacks from the South to the North. The continued influx of Puerto Ricans to Harlem. Two World Wars. The Harlem Renaissance. The black nationalist movement. The rise of ragtime, blues and jazz music. The rise of local political activism in both East and West Harlem. And amid this bustling community, individuals in Harlem were breaking barriers and making enormous strides on their own, and many of them were the first to make such achievements.

In virtually all aspects of life, whether it was the arts, business, politics or sports, someone from Harlem broke new ground in the area. The number of "firsts" associated with the artists of the Renaissance era and beyond is astounding. W.E.B. Du Bois' early writings would inspire many of the future Renaissance artists. For many of these artists, Du Bois' race consciousness through his writing and his spirit of self-determination and focus on the possibilities for African Americans was refreshing.

As the Renaissance and the arts community thrived in Harlem, new ground was also being broken with African American journalism and media ventures. The Harlem Broadcasting Corporation was established in 1929 and became the first black radio venture of its kind. It operated its own radio studios at Lenox Avenue and 125th Street in Harlem, leased time on local radio outlet WRNY and operated an artist bureau for black radio talent.[27] This station would be just one of a number of media outlets that would establish themselves with roots in Harlem, and many of them did so following World War I.

With the close of the war, out went most of the illusions and high hopes American Negroes had felt would be realized when it was seen that they were doing to the utmost their bit at home and in the field. Eight months after the armistice, with black men back fresh from the front, there broke the Red Summer of 1919, and the mingled emotions of the race were bitterness, despair and anger. There developed an attitude of cynicism that was a characteristic foreign to the Negro. There developed also a spirit of defiance born of desperation. These sentiments and reactions found varying degrees of expression in the Negro publications throughout the country, but Harlem became the center where they were formulated and voiced to the Negroes of America and the world. Radicalism in Harlem, which had declined as the war approached, burst out anew.

Perhaps no one had more or as fierce a race consciousness as Marcus Garvey, the native Jamaican who arrived in Harlem around 1916 intent on unifying black people worldwide. Garvey was committed to improving life for blacks worldwide by calling for unity and pride among the people. In 1914, he founded the Universal Negro Improvement Association (UNIA) in Jamaica, but in 1916, he moved the headquarters to New York City. Garvey's movement was significant in that nothing like it had ever been attempted on behalf of African Americans anywhere in the world.

Garvey's UNIA garnered thousands of supporters in Harlem and beyond. His movement was a significant moment for Harlem because in some ways it helped build upon the already growing sense of pride among black Harlem residents. Garvey, considered a "black nationalist," was an unwavering proponent of racial pride. He called for people of African descent worldwide to return to Africa to escape the racial oppression around the globe.

Marcus Garvey, the Jamaican-born founder of the United Negro Improvement Association. Garvey is known for his ideals advocating that people of African descent return to Africa.

Garvey's wife, Amy Jacques-Garvey, writes in the preface of Marcus Garvey's most recognized volume of works, *The Philosophy and Opinions of Marcus Garvey (or Africa for the Africans)*, vols. I and II:

> *This volume is compiled from the speeches and articles delivered and written by Marcus Garvey from time to time. My purpose for compiling same primarily, was not for publication, but rather to keep as a personal record of the opinions and sayings of my husband during his career as the leader of that portion of the human family known as the Negro Race. However, on second thought, I decided to publish this volume in order to give to the public an opportunity of studying and forming an opinion of him; not from inflated and misleading newspaper and magazine articles, but from expressions of thoughts enunciated by him in defence of his oppressed and struggling race; so that by his own words he may be judged, and Negroes the world over may be informed and inspired, for truth, brought to light, forces conviction, and a state of conviction inspires action.*
>
> *The history of contact between the white and black races for the last three hundred years or more, records only a series of pillages, wholesale murders, atrocious brutalities, industrial exploitation, disfranchisement of the one on the other; the strong against the weak; but the sun of evolution is gradually*

> rising, shedding its light between the clouds of misery and oppression, and quickening and animating to racial consciousness and eventual national independence black men and women the world over.
>
> *It is human, therefore, that few of us within the Negro race can comprehend this transcendent period. We all suffer in a more or less degree; we all feel this awakened spirit of true manhood and womanhood; but it is given to few the vision of leadership—it is an inspiration—it is a quality born in man. Therefore in the course of leadership it is natural that one should meet opposition because of ignorance, lack of knowledge and sympathy of the opposition in understanding fully the spirit of leadership.*

The volume itself includes pieces written by Marcus Garvey on topics entitled "Prejudice," "Radicalism," the "Fall of Governments," the "Cause of Wars," the "Image of God" and "The True Solution of the Negro Problem."

Marcus Garvey, in discussing the benefits of nationhood, writes, "Nationhood is the only means by which modern civilization can completely protect itself. Independence of nationality, independence of government, is the means of protecting not only the individual but the group. Nationhood is the highest ideal of all peoples." In 1924, thousands of people would line Harlem's streets for a UNIA parade.

Thousands marched through the streets of Harlem for a United Negro Improvement Association parade in 1924.

While Garvey's movement attracted many people, it did not attract the masses, and some viewed him as a "comical figure."[28] Nevertheless, in accordance with his basic goal of Negroes going back to Africa, he created a steamship company that would facilitate that goal; however, Garvey would eventually be imprisoned for fraud. He then returned to Jamaica and later died in London. Despite his inability to achieve the goal he set out to reach, Garvey is considered the leading figure of black nationalism.

In his 1988 book *A Hard Road to Glory*, the late tennis legend Arthur Ashe wrote about one of the first black basketball teams and its owner:

> *The New York Renaissance, better known as the Rens, began as the Spartan Braves of Brooklyn. The Spartan Braves became the Spartan Five, and later still became the Rens in 1923. The Braves had joined New York City's Metropolitan Basketball Association (MBA) but the MBA in 1922 ordered the Braves to suspend Frank Forties and Leon Monde for a violation. The Spartans refused and were fined. The following year, the Braves' owner, Robert J. Douglas took Forties and added four others to form the Rens. It was the first full-salaried, black professional basketball team. Full credit must go to Douglas, who is now referred to as the father of black basketball. His keen eye for talent and sound business acumen enabled his squad to survive until the late 1940s.*[29]

The team would eventually become known as the Harlem Rens.

However, when it comes to basketball and Harlem, only one team typically comes to mind—the Harlem Globetrotters. The team, which officially is a semipro team, has been entertaining crowds for decades and still tours to this day. However, most fans are probably unaware that the team is connected to Harlem, New York, in name only.

At just twenty-four years old, in 1926, Abe Saperstein formed a basketball team in Illinois called the Savoy Big Five. The team was named after Chicago's Savoy Ballroom, which patterned itself after New York City's famous ballroom of the same name. The first game the team played was on January 7, 1927, in Hinckley, Illinois. Players wore jerseys with the words "New York" printed on them to make others believe they were from the city. This gimmick would go on for a little while.

The Savoy Big Five's name eventually changed to Saperstein's New York Globetrotters and then to the Harlem, New York Globetrotters and finally the Harlem Globetrotters. Ironically, the team never actually played a game in Harlem, New York, until 1968.

The People of Harlem

About thirteen years after their beginnings in 1926, the team that most people recognize as the Harlem Globetrotters came into being. The Globetrotters played in their first professional basketball championship tournament in 1939. They lost to none other than the Harlem Rens. However, following that loss, the team would return to the championship, winning year after year.

The year 1939 also marks the time when the team began incorporating their comic antics into their games. Impromptu and unrehearsed, the antics began during a regular-season basketball game in which the Harlem Globetrotters led by the unbelievable score of 112 to 5. Bored, players on the team started being silly during the game. Crowds loved it and responded positively. After that, team owner Abe Saperstein endorsed the actions, and they have since been the team's gimmick.

Although the Harlem Globetrotters were not officially from Harlem, New York, they are beloved representatives. If one were speaking practically anywhere in the world about basketball players and simply said "the Globetrotters," few would not know that they are talking about the Harlem Globetrotters. In an ironic way, the team, which is formed primarily as an entertainment show, does represent something that many Harlemites seem to have a lot of—talent. Even though the Globetrotters place entertaining first, the team members are "real" basketball players with great talent in shooting and handling the basketball, which they use in their shows.

Another sports figure with great talent who came out of Harlem is none other than tennis player Althea Gibson. Gibson grew up in New York City and learned to play the game of tennis on the public courts at 155th Street. She started playing amateur tennis in the 1940s, and from 1950 to 1955, she enjoyed success at that level. Gibson was the dominant women's tennis player of the late '50s. She was the first African American player to win the French Open in 1956 and both the U.S. Open and Wimbledon in 1957. She then repeated both victories—the U.S. Open and Wimbledon—in 1958. In both 1957 and 1958, Althea Gibson was ranked number one in the world of tennis.

A phenomenal athlete, Gibson would win numerous titles in singles and doubles tennis in the late '50s. In 1957, the Associated Press named her Female Athlete of the Year. And she would not stop there. As a youth, Gibson had enjoyed tennis as well as golf. After her tennis career ended, Gibson continued to break sports barriers. In 1964, she became the first African American woman to play in the Ladies Professional Golf Association.

In East Harlem, just as African Americans were doing in West Harlem, Puerto Ricans and Italians were making gains in the political arena. When many Puerto Ricans first arrived in East Harlem, they brought with them the entrepreneurial skills that they were familiar with in their home state. Bodegas, the small neighborhood stores that fill East and West Harlem, and other businesses popped up throughout the community as new immigrants arrived. Eventually, the drive to start new businesses shifted to a desire to achieve political power.

Oscar Garcia Rivera was born in Mayguez, Puerto Rico, in 1900. He first came to New York City in 1917 and then returned in 1926. Several years later, in 1930, he graduated from St. John's University School of Law. Shortly after graduating from law school, Rivera opened up law offices across New York City, including one in East Harlem. In fact, Garcia was concerned about the poor, and in his East Harlem office, he offered pro bono work for residents who could not afford his services.

Numerous singers and entertainers created or participated in events that were "firsts" in Harlem. Nathaniel Coles, better known as Nat King Cole, led the first black jazz group to have its own sponsored program on radio in 1948. In the years following, he focused on his singing career, and by 1952, he was one of the most successful singers of popular music. In 1956 and 1957, he was the second black man to host a nationwide network television show.[30]

Lena Horne, the gorgeous singer and entertainer whose heyday was in the '30s and '40s, got her start in the entertainment business in Harlem. In 1933, Lena Horne had her very first professional audition at the Cotton Club. She was just sixteen years old.

The list of those who have made history "firsts" and who are in some way connected to Harlem, New York, extends well beyond the entertainment world. In fact, it reaches up into the upper echelon of the United States government. Civil War general and former U.S. president Ulysses S. Grant's burial tomb is located in Harlem, New York. When Grant took the oath of office on March 4, 1869, he was forty-six years old—the youngest president the United States had yet known.[31] Victorious in leading the Union army to defeat the Confederate army in the Civil War, President Grant would be active in protecting the rights of all Americans, including African Americans.

In 1870, during Reconstruction (the postwar period of rebuilding the South), U.S. Congress passed the Fifteenth Amendment, giving black men the right to vote. (Women still did not have the right to vote.) In December of that year, Senator Hiram Revels of Mississippi and Representative Joseph Rainey of South Carolina became the first African American men to serve in Congress. President Grant pushed former Confederate states to make sure their state governments upheld these new rights for African Americans.

He wanted to make sure these states observed all the laws of the United States, not just those that benefited whites.[32]

Ulysses S. Grant ran for reelection for president in 1872. He and his running mate, Senator Henry Wilson of Massachusetts, were victorious. However, Grant's vice president during his first term, Schuyler Colfax, could not run for a possible second term. In September 1872, news broke that Vice President Schuyler Colfax had received shares of Union Pacific Railroad stock when he was Speaker of the House of Representatives. The railroad stock was thought to have been a bribe to keep Colfax and other members of Congress from investigating the railroad's illegal financial schemes. Republicans refused to allow Colfax to run for reelection with Grant. The Credit Mobilier bribery scandal, as the Union Pacific deal was called, ruined Colfax, but President Grant's reputation remained clean.[33]

President Grant left office in March 1877. The years following his two terms as president he spent doing something he had always enjoyed. Ever since he was a child, Ulysses Grant had loved to travel and see new places. After he his wife, Julia, left the White House, they decided to tour the world. The couple spent two and a half years circling the globe with their teenage son, Jesse. Everywhere the Grants went, they were treated royally. Their thirty-month travels were paid for by Ulysses Grant's one good investment. Years earlier, Grant had bought shares in a mining operation that hit a rich vein of silver. When the money ran out, the Grants came home to the United States.[34]

During his era, as a former president, Grant was not entitled to a pension, so this meant that he would have to work in some capacity to create income for his family following his time in office. After starting an ill-fated investment firm with a financial star known as "the young Napoleon (emperor) of Wall Street," Ferdinand Ward, Grant ended up nearly destitute at sixty-two years old. When word of his situation spread, offers of support came in. This included money and checks as well as Civil War–related offers to display his memorabilia. The latter offers he declined. Most of Grant's military possessions—uniforms, swords and trophies—were given in a trust to the government. They ended up at West Point (where he attended) and the Smithsonian Institution, a national museum.[35]

Grant spent his final years as a writer producing articles about Civil War battles for *Century Magazine*. At one point, the magazine's editors asked him about producing a book, but with no guarantee that he would be paid. When Grant's friend, famed writer Mark Twain, found out what the editors were suggesting, he convinced Grant that he deserved more. Twain offered to publish Grant's book and give him generous profits. Financially, Grant

Grant's tomb postcard.

again made a comeback when, in March 1885, Congress decided to give him his rank and salary as a general of the army, which he had to give up as president. Although he was retired, he would once again receive his full military salary.

Ulysses Grant learned that he had throat cancer right before he agreed to work on his memoir for Mark Twain. Determined and committed to put his story down on paper, he wrote courageously as he fought the illness that would take his life. On July 16, 1885, he declared himself done with his memoir. Just a week after finishing his book, Ulysses S. Grant died quietly in his sleep. And this final achievement—the completion of his memoirs—itself would make history.

Ulysses S. Grant was the first U.S. president to publish a book about his experience. Grant's memoirs, titled *The Personal Memoirs of U.S. Grant*, sold more than 300,000 copies, and it is still considered one of the finest books on American military history. Two years after publication, Mark Twain presented Julia with a check for $200,000. Eventually, Grant's book would bring his family more than $450,000.[36]

Upon his death, Grant's family requested that he have a military funeral in the state of New York. On the day of the funeral, thousands of people lined the streets and walked uptown to pay their respects. Ulysses S. Grant was laid to rest in Riverside Park at 122nd Street and Riverside Drive. Grant's

The People of Harlem

tomb overlooks the Hudson River and is located in the Morningside Heights section of Harlem. For the last five years of his life, former president and general Ulysses S. Grant lived in New York City. He requested to be buried in the city. Today, the General Grant National Memorial, or Grant's Tomb, as it is commonly referred to, "is not only the final resting place of the General but a memorial to his life and accomplishments."[37] The site is monitored by the National Park Service and is open to the public daily.

During its jazz and arts heyday in the 1920s and '30s, Harlem streets were full of dance clubs, theaters and other nightspots, and the people who wanted to fill them up. Nightclubs such as the Club Sudan, Jock's Place and Club Baron were all over Harlem. Club Baron was located at 132nd and Lenox and was considered one of the most sophisticated and luxurious black clubs in the nation.[38]

Club-goers included both those who just wanted to have a good time as well as those who were in the entertainment business and looking for that big break. For many, whether it was singing or playing music, that break would come somewhere on a Harlem, New York stage.

Both legendary singers Ella Fitzgerald and Billie Holiday started their singing careers in Harlem. And both would have their share of hardship before becoming widely successful. Born in Newport News, Virginia, Fitzgerald grew up in Yonkers, New York. After her mother died in 1932, Fitzgerald had to live in an orphanage before going to live with an aunt in Harlem while in her mid-teens. She

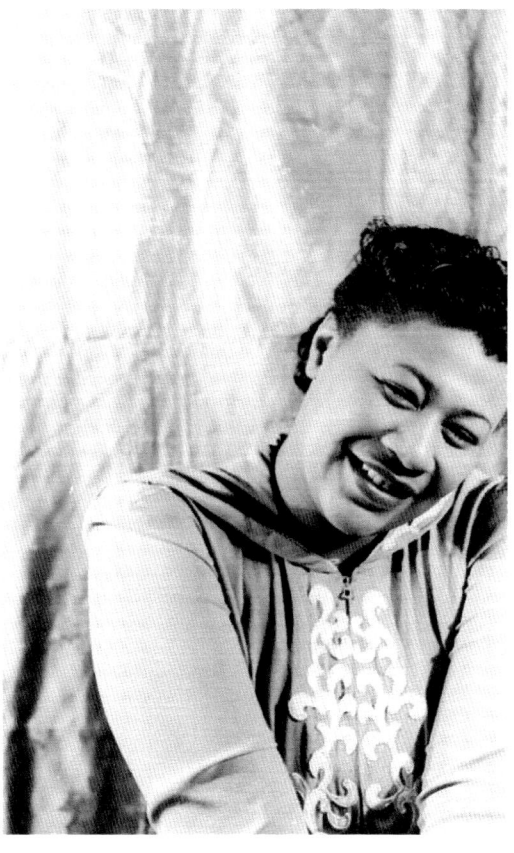

Legendary jazz singer Ella Fitzgerald, who began singing in clubs in Harlem.

and her sister Frances were "shuttled in and out of relatives' flats and Harlem foster homes. More than once Ella ran away from intolerable situations to fend for herself. Tall, gawky and haphazardly dressed, the adolescent Ella was no harbinger of the elegant, mature gentlewoman she would become. She aspired to be a famous dancer. From the age of eight, she had danced in the streets with her peers, begging older children to teach her such tap steps as the fast-traveling 'Shuffle Off to Buffalo' and novelty dances the rugcutters at the Savoy Ballroom were into."[39]

Ella Fitzgerald jumpstarted her amazing career in Harlem after struggling for a while to make it in the business. Allegedly, on more than one occasion early on in her career, her appearance, which some said was disheveled, thwarted her chance to succeed. One of her first experiences with this attitude was reportedly at the world-famous Apollo Theatre. It cost her an amateur night victory. But just down the street a little bit, her opportunity and her day to shine would come.

The Harlem Opera House opened under new management in June 1934. Just doors away from the Apollo, the new owners, Leo Brecker and Frank Schiffman, wanted to give the Apollo a run for its money. It was partly the success of the Apollo that had caused the Lafayette —also run by Brecker and Schiffman—to fold. The Harlem Opera House started holding an almost identical amateur night —with the same promise of a gig as the main prize—on Tuesday nights. In January 1935, Ella took her shot on the Harlem Opera House stage and brought the house down once again. Her first-prize win was even mentioned in the *New York Age*—the first time her name ever appeared in the paper.[40]

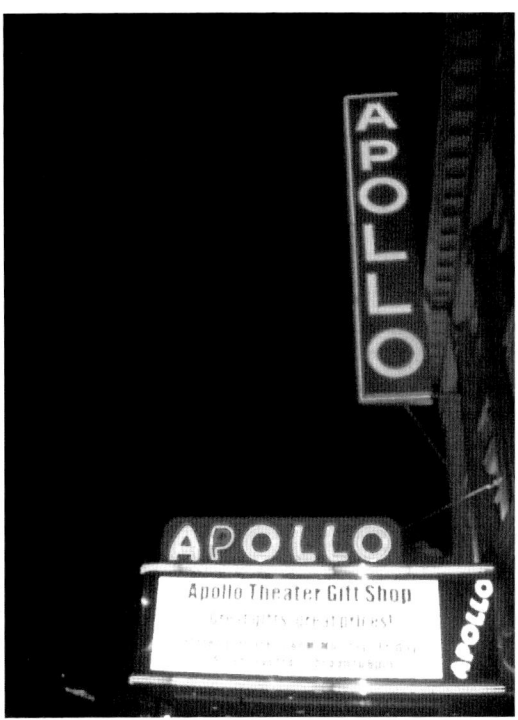

One of Harlem's most recognizable buildings, the Apollo Theater.

The People of Harlem

Billie Holiday also started her career singing around clubs in Harlem. Like Ella Fitzgerald, Billie's childhood was affected by poverty and abuse. In the 1930s, Holiday toured with Count Basie's and Artie Shaw's bands. Much in the style of her friend and collaborator, the Basie saxophonist Lester Young, Holiday projected a quiet, smoky-sounding and introspective voice that was limited in its range of notes but deeply expressive.[41]

Over the course of her career, Holiday would gain the reputation for doing "message songs," and none was more powerful than 1939's "Strange Fruit." The song was a "searing indictment" of lynching in the South. At one Manhattan nightclub that was a gathering place for white and black artists and intellectuals, the song became a regular staple of entertainment. However, it would be Holiday's rendition of "God Bless the Child" for which she will forever be known.

Singer Ethel Waters arrived in New York City during World War I. She first recorded in 1921. On her early sessions, she sang with noted artists such as Fletcher Henderson, Coleman Hawkins, James P. Johnson and Duke Ellington. In 1927, she debuted on Broadway as the lead in the all-black production of *Africana*. Several years later, in 1933, Waters was singing "Stormy Weather" at the Cotton Club when songwriter Irving Berlin heard her and invited her to be in his play *As Thousands Cheer*. Waters would go on to appear in a number of stage, film and television productions for the next thirty years. Two of the songs that she is best known for performing are "Stormy Weather," a 1933 song by Harold Arlen; and "Harlem on My Mind," a 1933 song by Irving Berlin.[42]

Like several other pop music innovators of her

BILLIE HOLIDAY TO BE FEATURED IN ALL-WHITE BAND

Former Singer With Count Basie, Signed By Artie Shaw, Becomes Second Race Girl Holding Such a Spot.

NEW YORK, March 17—Billie Holiday, who ranks third on the top list of the nation's singers of swing songs, this week moves into history-making channels of colored theatricals, having become the second colored girl to be chosen to feature in an all-white band. Signed last week, Miss Holiday departed for Boston last Saturday, where she will join the all-white aggregation of Artie Shaw, who, this week, opened a three months engagement at the Roseland State Ballroom there. The contract given Billie to act as a part of this 'outfit is an indefinite one, and unless racial prejudices intervene, she will remain with the band from now on.

The organization which Miss Holiday has now become a part of is well known in the musical world, having featured many of the country's largest nite clubs and hotels from coast to coast, and a best seller on wax. Billie Holliday just recently completed a long-term engagement as featured vocalist with Count Basie and his orchestra, which has harried every important dance music spot in the country. With the group, she gained nation-wide favor for herself, and just last season was rated third among the best delineators of swing songs in the country.

Starting her first engagement with the band Monday last, and has already started in a groove that is the love of every swing cat in the land, and according to Boston's music critics, she is bound to prove a great asset to the ofay group.

Featured thusly, she becomes the second colored girl to be used as a permanent feature of a white band. June Richmond, with Jimmie Dorsey's band, is the only other. Theatrical circles look upon this new move as both a great break for the girl swinger and the entire world of colored entertainment.

A 1938 newspaper ad announcing Billie Holiday signing with Artie Shaw's band. Note the references to race in the article.

day, Ethel Waters led a desperately bleak early life. She was born in the poorest neighborhood of Chester, Pennsylvania, a southwestern suburb of Philadelphia, on Halloween night in 1896. During her career, she would gain a reputation of being tough and sometimes highly critical of those who could be considered her competition. However, Waters would overcome her troubled early life through grit and the application of her great talent.[43]

After singing jazz for most of her career, including regular show-stopping performances of "Stormy Weather" at Harlem's Cotton Club during the 1930s, she sang with evangelist Billy Graham from 1960 to 1975. Waters is considered one of the first black singers to achieve widespread popularity and also was among the first to blend jazz and popular music.[44]

The list of "Harlem firsts" is long and seems to constantly grow. In January 2010, Harlem had the special honor of being the place in Manhattan where the first baby of the year was born. Thyme Eva Rogers was born at Lenox Hill Hospital—just as the famous ball dropped in Times Square, ushering in the new year.[45]

David Dinkins

David Norman Dinkins was born on July 10, 1927, in Trenton, New Jersey. As a young boy, his family moved to Harlem, New York. At age six, his parents separated, and Dinkins returned to New Jersey as a teenager to live with his father. He eventually served in the U.S. Marine Corps during World War II. At the time, the Marine Corps was considered one of the most segregated branches of the American military.[46]

After the war, Dinkins moved on with his life and attended Howard University in Washington, D.C., an elite historically black college, where he majored in mathematics. He graduated in 1950 and returned to New York City. Several years later, he met his future wife, Joyce Burrows, and in 1953, they were married. Burrows is the daughter of a Harlem politician.

Dinkins continued with his schooling and attended Brooklyn Law School, graduating in 1956. He then returned to Harlem to practice law along with Fritz W. Alexander. In the years following law school, Dinkins forayed into politics. He participated in the George Washington Carver Club, which was led by New York City councilman J. Raymond "the Fox" Jones and Percy Sutton, a Harlem businessman and mentor for future congressman Adam Clayton Powell Jr. It would be Councilman Jones who would urge

Dinkins to run for New York State Assembly in 1965. In fact, Jones would become a pioneer in Harlem politics. Jones helped guide a number of Harlem politicians—David Dinkins included—to success in high-profile political positions.

Dinkins won the State Assembly race in 1965, and in 1967, he became the Harlem Democratic district leader. He served just one term in the New York State Assembly. Several years later, in 1972, Dinkins was elected the first black president of the Board of Elections. He went on to acquire another first in the city of New York. In 1989, he defeated former New York mayor Edward Koch in the Democratic primary. He went on to defeat Republican Rudolph Giuliani in the general election to become New York City's first African American mayor. Dinkins served just one term, ironically losing the next mayoral race in 1993 to the same man he had beat four years earlier—Rudolph Giuliani.

COLIN POWELL

Colin Powell was born in Harlem and had a distinguished military career before being selected as the sixty-fifth secretary of state for the United States by former president George W. Bush. Powell was the first African American to serve in that role. He served as secretary of state from 2001 to 2005.

A retired four-star army general, Powell held several high-ranking military positions before becoming the U.S. secretary of state. He also served as the national security advisor from 1987 to 1989. In addition, in 1989, he was also the commander in chief of the U.S. Army Forces Command.

Colin Powell would achieve another high-level military first. From 1989 to 1993, during the Gulf War, he was the chairman of the Joint Chiefs of Staff. He remains the first and only African American to serve on the Joint Chiefs of Staff.

Although his family moved from Harlem while he was a young boy, before launching his military career, Powell returned to Harlem to attend the City College of New York, where he earned a bachelor of science degree in geology in 1958. And even though he and his family have not lived in Harlem for many years, he has frequently acknowledged his connection to Harlem and has been a role model for many people in Harlem and beyond.

W.E.B. Du Bois

William Edward Burghardt—or W.E.B., as he is most commonly known—Du Bois is considered the elder statesman on political thought affecting the African American community. As a leading intellectual, his work and ideas have become the seminal model for political progression. He was both prolific and renowned for his intellect on social issues. Born in 1869 in Great Barrington, Massachusetts, he studied at Fisk University in Nashville, Tennessee, and Harvard University. Du Bois was the first African American to be awarded a PhD from Harvard, which he received in 1895.

In his classic 1903 book *The Souls of Black Folks*, Du Bois declared that "the problem of the twentieth century was the problem of the color line." His words would be referred to over and over again as historians, writers and social scientists who have come along after Du Bois address social issues of today.

Du Bois was the leading intellectual on political issues affecting African Americans, and many political and historical figures who followed him would look to Du Bois and his ideas and incorporate them into their own political philosophies. Du Bois spent many years living and working in Harlem.

W.E.B. Du Bois—sociologist, historian, author and the man considered to be the leading African American intellectual of his time—was also for many years a Harlem resident.

The People of Harlem

SHOWBIZ IN HARLEM

The list of celebrities—singers, musicians, athletes or actors and actresses—who have made Harlem part of their lives is long and reads like a who's who in entertainment. Some were born and raised in Harlem, and others came from afar and made Harlem home, but all of them helped make Harlem the special place that it is. Many of these entertainers have started at Harlem's famed Apollo Theater and gone on to have legendary careers with worldwide recognition. World-famous boxers Muhammad Ali and Joe Louis held boxing matches in Harlem venues early in their careers. Aretha Franklin, James Brown, Billie Holiday, Stevie Wonder, Ella Fitzgerald, Lena Horne and Michael Jackson are just a few of the numerous celebrities who once spent some time performing and/or socializing in Harlem.

And for those who have come through Harlem starting careers from the ground up, the Harlem community does not forget those stars it helps to create. When James Brown died in Atlanta on Christmas Day 2006, a memorial service was held at the famous Apollo Theater, where he performed early in his career. A white, horse-drawn carriage carried his body through the neighborhood that helped give him his start, and thousands lined the streets to pay their last respects and to reminiscence. Many other famous names would show up to pay their respects. This included the late King of Pop, Michael Jackson, whose own untimely death on June 25, 2009, at the age of fifty would spark a similar response by Harlem residents.

The shocking news of the King of Pop's sudden death stunned the world. In Harlem, people reportedly filled the streets crying, dancing, reminiscing

When he was not in the ring, boxer Joe Louis spent a lot of time socializing in Harlem.

and playing some of his numerous hits. Through the first days that followed news of his death, on 125th Street—the heart of Harlem—crowds gathered in front of the famed Apollo Theater. Many who were in the neighborhood at the time the news broke were notified of Jackson's death when the Apollo Theater changed its marquee to remember Michael Jackson. It read, "In Memory of Michael Jackson: A True Apollo Legend, 1958–2009." As a member of the Jackson Five, Michael Jackson and his famous brothers first won an amateur night competition at the theater in August 1967.

"Almost 2,000 fans clogged 125th Street in Harlem and held an impromptu memorial to Jackson. They moonwalked beneath the distinctive neon sign of the Apollo Theater and sang some of Jackson's greatest hits including 'Man in the Mirror' and 'Billie Jean.'"[47] The Apollo Theatre also set up a banner wall where fans could sign and leave messages for Michael and his family. Tour buses stopped to let tourists off the buses so they could sign the wall and join the hundreds of local fans who gathered throughout the day and night once the news was confirmed. Days after the news, motorcycle enthusiasts from New York City–area motorcycle clubs put on a "parade of bikes," riding down 125th Street in Harlem in front of the Apollo Theater as hundreds of fans and tourists filled the streets cheering in appreciation for the clubs' recognition of Jackson. Virtually every motorcycle club in the area was represented in the parade.

On July 7, 2009, at the Staples Center in Los Angeles, the world watched as one of the most spectacular memorial services the public has ever seen was held to honor Michael Jackson and his tremendous contributions to pop culture. After a private service for the family, Michael Jackson's body was laid in a gold casket covered with roses as many pillars of the music industry—Berry Gordy, founder of Motown, Smokey Robinson, Stevie Wonder—praised his talent and humanitarianism in front of nearly 20,000 people. The service, however, was broadcast around the world, and it was estimated that well over 200 million people viewed it. In August 2009, the Apollo Theater announced that it would induct Michael Jackson posthumously into its Legends Hall of Fame.

The renowned Apollo Theater, still thriving as much today as it did years ago, is just one of a number of venues and theaters that once lined the streets of Harlem. Opened in 1935 by Frank Schiffman and Leo Brecher, the four-story building was originally constructed for the old Hurtig Seamon burlesque theater in 1904.[48]

Just a few doors down the block from the Apollo was the Harlem Opera House. It was here that jazz phenomenon Ella Fitzgerald had a public breakthrough. "The first time Ella's name appeared in an ad was on a February 15, 1935, Harlem Opera House revue poster."[49] Oscar Hammerstein opened the Harlem Opera House in 1889 in the hope that middle-class families would move to Harlem in large numbers.

Cab Calloway, the flamboyant singer known for his zoot suits and animated gestures on stage, became a regular at the famed Hotel Theresa, but prior to that, he ignited another Harlem hotel with his performances. There were no clean, respectable hotels for blacks in Harlem in the 1930s. A number of musicians reluctantly stayed at Love B. Wood's Woodside Hotel on Lenox Avenue and 147th Street, despite its unsavory reputation. The hit song "Jumping at the Woodside" by Cab Calloway made the hotel a popular hangout for musicians and the fast crowd.[50] Calloway is most known for his catchy "hi di hi di hi di ho" hook on one of his most famous songs, "Minnie the Moocher."

Just as jazz and literature dominated the 1930s, so did fashion. And Cab Calloway was influential in this area too. Trumpet player Joe Wilder recalled, "Cab Calloway made the zoot suit a fad in the late 1930s. That zoot suit had the peg-leg pant that widened above the knee. Then there was the long coat with a hemline that hit around the knee. The zoot suit was definitely colorful too."[51]

While jazz was lighting up the town in Harlem, other artists who were not musicians or singers were filling up their pages with words, painting their canvases, jumping into character and dancing their steps.

As vibrantly as Cab Calloway rocked Harlem stages, legendary singer and actress Lena Horne illuminated Harlem's Cotton Club as one of the club's renowned showgirls and dancers. Horne would eventually go on to mega success as a singer and Hollywood actress. Widely known for her stunning beauty, Lena Horne was also known for being outspoken on social issues at a time when many other blacks were not. Although outspoken, Horne had much success as an actress, and through the 1930s and 1940s, she starred in a number of films and productions, most notably *Stormy Weather*, the 1943 film that featured other stars such as Cab Calloway and his band, dancer Bill Robinson, Katherine Dunham and her dance troupe, the famous Nicholas Brothers and musician Fats Waller. Horne's rendition of the song "Stormy Weather" is a classic and is considered her signature song.

Some of the painters who were part of the Harlem Renaissance along with the prolific Aaron Douglas include Palmer Hayden, William H. Johnson and Malvin Gray Johnson. Douglas was a well-known figure and sought-after talent during the Renaissance. His illustrations appeared in books such as James Weldon Johnson's *God's Trombones: Seven Negro Sermons in Verse* and Alain Locke's *The New Negro*. Douglas also did cover art work for *Opportunity* and *Crisis* magazines of the NAACP and the Urban League.

Countless movies and books have been based in Harlem or have had storylines involving Harlem. Whether the story is about real events or is fiction, the allure from Harlem's Renaissance era, the cultural center for African Americans for decades, still lives. The "world's best-known neighborhood," as some have called Harlem, has inspired many films, books and characters with connections to Harlem. In fact, the world of comic art has a long history of characters rooted in Harlem. "In the superhero genre, the first mainstream black superhero was the Black Panther, an African King named T'Challa, created by Marvel Comics in 1966. For a period, T'Challa functioned as a Harlem schoolteacher."[52]

For many years, Harlem was a playground for the famous and well connected. And as the entertainment world's elite mixed and mingled, so did the elite members of the sports world, especially the boxers. The legendary Jack Johnson, Joe Louis and Muhammad Ali all have come through Harlem. Johnson was also a business owner—one of the original owners of the world-famous Cotton Club—and Louis and Ali spent time socializing in Harlem early in their careers. Louis would often stay at the Hotel Theresa, and when he won some of his most famous boxing matches, Harlem celebrated.

Jack Johnson, the infamous and fearless boxer known for his independent attitude, was at one time a part owner of the Cotton Club.

The People of Harlem

Harlem Renaissance

The Harlem Renaissance is likely the most famous period in Harlem's history. During this period in the 1920s and 1930s, numerous writers, poets and other artists flocked to the area, creating an outpouring of artistic and professional works without precedent in the American black community. Music, art, theater and literature were all made in Harlem, and major artists were established in every genre.

Known primarily for its writers, the Renaissance included music and dance, theater and visual artists such as Romare Bearden and Aaron Douglas, one of the most prolific artists and illustrators during the Renaissance era. Douglas did the artwork for the projects of a number of Renaissance-era artists. Today, at the Harlem YMCA on 135th Street, some of his painted works remain and a room is named in his honor. This particular YMCA was the site of many meetings and gatherings of Renaissance artists and has been named a historical landmark. Josephine Baker, who started dancing

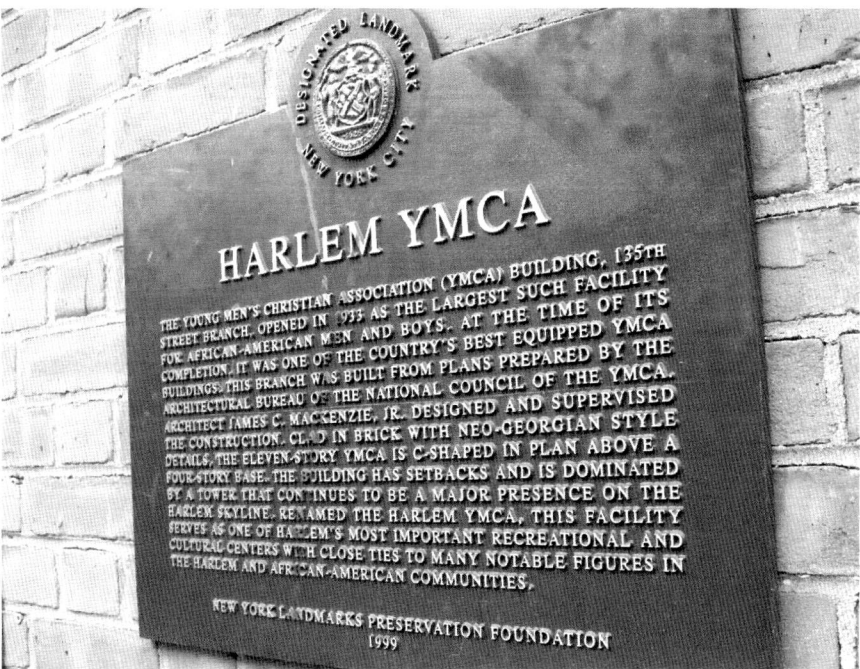

New York Landmarks Preservation Foundation sign designating the 135th Street Harlem YMCA a landmark. The building was the site of many meetings of Harlem Renaissance–era artists.

Singer and dancer Josephine Baker was one of many performers who made stops in Harlem. Baker, however, became disgruntled in America and moved to Paris, where she remained for the rest of her life.

at Harlem's Cotton Club during Harlem's Renaissance, eventually left Harlem to live and work in Paris, where she received worldwide accolades for her dancing and singing. Baker enjoyed overwhelming success in Paris, where she lived most of her life.

Though the visual arts often have not gotten as much attention as other areas of the Renaissance, clearly the advances in recognition and respect that visual artists achieved was unprecedented in the white, elitist world of modern art at the time. Through their art, these artists put America on notice that black themes—the lives, activities and portraits of African Americans—were a legitimate, valuable and unique part of American life and that black artists deserved recognition and patronage equal to any other artist.[53]

Langston Hughes, one of the most prolific writers of the Renaissance era, called Harlem home. For many years, he resided at 20 East 127th Street in East Harlem. A few of his most well-known poems are "The Weary Blues," "Harlem" and "I've Known Rivers." Part of what is so amazing about his literary output is not just the volume of work but the many different genres that he wrote in. Hughes, who grew up in the Midwest and arrived in New York City to attend Columbia University, wrote poems, short stories, radio shows, operas and more. Of all the Renaissance writers, Hughes was unquestionably the most prolific. He was part of a core group of Renaissance-era writers that included Countee Cullen, James Weldon Johnson, Claude McKay, Zora Neale Hurston and Wallace Thurman. The work of Langston Hughes has had a powerful and lasting impact on African Americans.

Langston Hughes's most famous character, Jesse B. Semple, still "lives" on stages across the United States through the work of one New York–

The People of Harlem

based actor, Anthony Thompson. Hughes's Semple represents a sort of "urban everyman"—neither highly educated nor rich yet his voice is representative of a segment of the collective African American community. Thompson, a native of Pittsburgh, developed a stage show, *Langston Hughes's Jesse B. Simple: Alive in Harlem*, which he says "reintroduces Langston Hughes's character to the community of Harlem and celebrates the *Simple Tales*." Through appearances at community centers, churches, coffee houses and other locations, Thompson portrays Jesse B. in a solo performance.

In Thompson's project overview, he writes:

Nella Larsen was a Renaissance-era writer most known for her books *Passing* and *Quicksand*. She eventually moved away from writing and pursued other interests.

> *On February 13, 1943, Hughes introduced Jesse B. to the readers of his weekly column in the black-owned* Chicago Defender, *depicting him as an ordinary Harlem resident who over a glass of beer expresses his views on religion, politics, social issues and being black in America. This winning character became so popular that in 1950 Hughes edited selections from his columns and published them in a book form as* Simple Tales. *Jesse B. Simple, who had endured the horrors of Jim Crow in the South before migrating to Harlem, did much more than survive the voice of Harlem, a man with racial pride, dignity and respect. As a child, he felt that he belonged to nobody because he was "passed around," but despite his despair Jesse B. Simple becomes a hero. He tells his tales with humor, but sometimes they hit as sharp as the corns on his feet. His straightforward views and solutions to the world's problems have won him recognition as a repository of African-American wisdom.*

One of the premier women of the Renaissance, Zora Neale Hurston, arrived in Harlem from Jacksonville, Florida. Most recognized for her classic work *Their Eyes Were Watching God*, Hurston wrote several other novels, including *Jonah's Gourd Vine*, *Moses, Man of the Mountain* and *Seraph on the Suwanee*. When the Harlem Renaissance began to fade, Hurston returned to Jacksonville and lived almost as a recluse until she died.

One of the leading members of Harlem's Renaissance was James Weldon Johnson. A teacher and writer, Johnson was born in Jacksonville, Florida. In New York, he would become a central figure of the era. He arrived in New York City at the beginning of the twentieth century in 1901.

James Weldon Johnson grew up in a family that nurtured his artistic bent and introduced him to languages, literature and music at an early age. This early introduction set the foundation for his life, which would take the path of both political activist and commentator and successful songwriter. Johnson graduated from Atlanta University in 1894, and shortly afterward, he was appointed principal of the Stanton School in Jacksonville.

Just three years after he graduated from Atlanta University, James Weldon Johnson founded the first high school for blacks in the state of Florida; became the first black lawyer to pass the Florida bar exam; and founded and edited the *Daily American*, the first daily newspaper for black Americans. In 1900, he found time to write the lyrics to the Negro national anthem, "Lift Every Voice and Sing."[54] Johnson would author two titles, *The Autobiography of an Ex-Colored Man* in 1912 and *Black Manhattan* in 1930, which are considered classics and can be seen in college classrooms across the country today.

Countee Cullen, a poet, writer and teacher during the Renaissance era, was among the array of writers and artists producing work at the time. In 1924, he published the novel *One Way to Heaven*, and in 1925, Harper and Brothers published his book of poetry, *Color*. Unlike most of the other artists from the Harlem Renaissance era who migrated to Harlem from other parts of the country,

James Weldon Johnson wrote the song "Lift Every Voice and Sing," which is considered the "Negro anthem." His many other works include poetry and the classic book *Black Manhattan*.

Cullen grew up in the area. He would publish several other titles before turning to teaching, which he did for many years. Today, a library and a school in Harlem are named in his honor.

Writers and poets were not the only artists who participated in the Harlem Renaissance. Photographers and painters were also creating the numerous works revered around the world to this day. Famed photographer James Van Der Zee, who is known for his portraits, opened his first photography studio at 135th Street and Lenox Avenue in Harlem. At one time, he served as the official photographer for black nationalist Marcus Garvey.

But beyond his own photographic work, Van Der Zee can be credited with helping to ensure that the legacy of all Harlem artists lived on. During the late '60s, Van Der Zee worked with New York's Metropolitan Museum of Art on an exhibition entitled "Harlem on My Mind," which recorded sixty years of life in Harlem. Van Der Zee was the largest contributor to the exhibit, which opened in 1969 and brought him international acclaim. The following year, the museum bought sixty of his images to add to its permanent collection. In addition, the museum established an institute in his name to promote the work of young minority photographers.[55]

Painter Romare Bearden was the son of a well-known political activist and a newspaper editor in Harlem and became acquainted with many of Harlem's artists, such as Langston Hughes, as a youth. In the '30s, he studied and developed his art before hosting his own exhibitions. Through various artist organizations, Bearden remained connected to fellow Harlem artists and, in the '60s, was appointed the art director of the Harlem Cultural Council.

Many of Harlem's Renaissance writers and artists were aided in their careers by whites who were friends of the artists and supportive of their work. For Langston Hughes in particular, Carl Van Vechten was a New York socialite whom Hughes befriended and whom he would remain friends with throughout his career. Van Vechten was a writer and photographer himself, but he developed an interest in promoting black art and culture. He was a frequent participant in the Harlem arts scene, and over the years, he was supportive and helpful to Hughes on many occasions. But it was one of Van Vechten's literary works that would keep both "white New York" and "black New York" talking.

Carl Van Vechten authored a very successful and controversial novel, *Nigger Heaven*, about black life in Harlem. The book's title refers to the balcony seating area in many theaters where blacks were restricted to sit for many years—if they were allowed entry at all.

Carl Van Vechten was a staunch supporter of Renaissance-era artists, notably Langston Hughes, whose career he assisted for many years.

By the mid-1920s, Harlem was noted for its nightlife. It provided entertainment and amusement not only for its own residents but for white New Yorkers who traveled uptown for music, speakeasies and a taste of exotic Harlem after dark. Carl Van Vechten helped popularize Harlem, both through *Nigger Heaven* and informal tours of Harlem's clubs and cabarets he organized for his white friends. By the second half of the decade, the white crowds were coming on their own to mingle with blacks in the clubs of Jungle Alley or the Savoy or to hear top entertainment in all-white establishments like the Cotton Club.[56]

The Great Depression ravaged Harlem and silenced many of its creative voices. Tuberculosis and too much gin cut Wallace Thurman's life short in 1924. James Weldon Johnson died in 1938. Nella Larsen, author of *Passing* and *Quicksand*, moved to Brooklyn and lived in a mysterious, obscure manner. The legendary Zora Neale Hurston returned to her native Florida and lived like a semi-recluse. Poet Jean Toomer immersed himself in religious mysticism. And Jessie Fauset, Charles S. Johnson, Countee Cullen and Arna Bontemps devoted themselves full time to teaching. Of the Harlem Renaissance writers, only Langston Hughes remained visible after the 1930s ended.[57]

The same neighborhood that offered so much promise and hope to black Americans would ultimately turn into a place of widespread destitution during the Great Depression. The community that once was home to showgirls and "Thursday girls"—the name given to the many black women who worked in the homes of whites and were given Thursday as a day off—became a congested neighborhood where actual living space was tight and the means to survive was even tighter. "Before the full effects of the Depression were felt, the average weekly income of a Negro working man had been eighteen dollars. Sixty per cent of the married women worked, a figure four times higher than that of the native-born white Americans."[58]

What also helped to make these years especially tough for the people of Harlem was the density of the community. Since so many people had flocked to the area because of its allure, Harlem's apartments and homes were packed with people. As wages and opportunities dwindled, many artists of the era resorted to other means to make a living while the rest of Harlem's overcrowded community concentrated on basic survival.

However, the suffering of Harlem artists during the Depression was just a microcosm of what was happening throughout the community. While Harlem was known for its glistening entertainment, the masses of community residents were just getting by. Men and women worked, but most often, these were in low-paying service jobs.

At any given time during the 1930s, a majority of Harlem families contained at least one working member whose employment opportunities were dramatically affected by the Great Depression. The black occupational structure had changed since the 1920s, generally to the detriment of black workers. African American economic opportunities, always limited, narrowed still further. While black skilled, unskilled and white-collar workers, men and women, and the foreign-born and native-born experienced these changes in different ways, all shared this shrinking of opportunity and the consequent low wages.[59]

POLITICAL ACTIVISTS AND POLITICIANS

Just as Harlem is recognized for its arts and culture, it is also known as "the spiritual home of the Negro protest movement."[60] Although the people and the politics of the mid-twentieth century are recognized for their achievements, political activism in Harlem was definitely alive and well as early as the 1920s. And there was one man who especially shocked and stunned America not just by his political voice but also by his precise political actions. While he and his philosophies shook much of America, these same philosophies buoyed and invigorated black America. Marcus Garvey and his politics would move like a whirlwind through Harlem and shake the United States.

Born in Jamaica in 1887, intelligent but unschooled, a newspaper writer in Jamaica and Costa Rica, short, chunky and mustached Garvey came to Harlem in 1917. The next year, he began publishing a weekly called the *Negro World* in which he urged Negro unity, nationalism and the resettlement of Negroes in Africa. He appealed to racial pride at a time when Negroes felt that they had little cause to hold up their heads. A skilled orator, clever organizer and shrewd psychologist, Garvey touched off the first real mass movement among American Negroes.[61]

Between 1919 and 1921, Garvey collected $10 million. In 1923, he claimed 6 million followers. This was an exaggeration, but even his critics admitted that 500,000 Negroes had pledged blind loyalty to him. Garvey set up two steamship companies and bought three seagoing ships in the name of his Universal Negro Improvement Association. He intended to man the vessels with Negro crews and sail from the United States to Africa and the West Indies. However, Garvey's fate would change in 1923 when he was found guilty of using the mail to defraud in raising money for his steamship lines and was sent to the federal penitentiary at Atlanta for five years. President Calvin Coolidge pardoned him but had him deported as an undesirable man. Marcus Garvey died in London in 1940.[62] Although he died outside the country, the people of Harlem certainly never forgot his impact and his goal for people of African descent. Upon his death, a massive remembrance was held in New York City in his honor.

Adam Clayton Powell Jr. led the charge in giving Harlem its reputation as a political power base. The son of a preacher who led Abyssinian Baptist Church for decades, Adam Jr. took it to the streets of Harlem before becoming an elected official. It was Powell who led a campaign in the 1930s to urge African Americans to "not buy where you can't work." He would lead marchers in protests carrying signs walking up and down the sidewalks of 125th Street. The target of one of these campaigns was Blumstein's Department Store, which was considered an "uptown Saks store." This was especially important because the store was located right along the main strip of

Marcus Garvey Memorial flyer.

the Harlem community. Blacks, more often than not, were unable to work at many of the established businesses. Blumstein's eventually changed its policy, and today, while the store is gone, the old "Blumstein's" sign remains.

Adam Clayton Powell Jr. was politically active for most of his life. He graduated from Colgate University in 1930 and immediately became an assistant pastor at his father's church. He would go on to earn a master's degree in religious education from Teacher's College in 1932 and a doctor of divinity degree from Shaw University in 1938. As assistant pastor, he oversaw employment and education programs, as well as a soup kitchen at Abyssinian, before taking his father's position as pastor.

In addition to his work with the church, his community activism magnified throughout Harlem and beyond. Powell became legendary. He helped to establish the Equal Employment Coordinating Committee while vigorously continuing to lead boycotts against companies that excluded blacks.

In 1941, Powell became the first black member of New York's city council. Several years later, in 1944, he was elected to represent a newly drawn Harlem district in Congress where blacks were the majority. For more than twenty years, he worked tirelessly on legislation to improve housing, education and civil rights.

The Adam Clayton Powell Jr. State Office Building on 125th Street houses offices for a number of Harlem-focused organizations, as well as New York state businesses.

A Harlem resident on Adam Clayton Powell Boulevard.

During his lifetime, Powell could often be seen walking among various protesters—his own protest sign in hand—rallying with workers fighting for equal rights or standing at a podium rallying a group of people. Today, at the corner of 125th Street and Seventh Avenue, the avenue now bears his name, Adam Clayton Powell Jr. Boulevard. In addition, a state office building also bearing his name commands one corner, along with a statue in his image paying tribute. Inside the building sits the Harlem Visitor Information Kiosk, which is staffed by knowledgeable personnel ready to help newcomers make their way around Harlem.

Paving the way for Powell and many other ranking politicians from Harlem was the "Harlem Fox," J. Raymond Jones. Jones, a native of St. Thomas, Virgin Islands, would establish one of the most powerful and prominent black political organizations in New York City. Considered a superb strategist, in the 1920s and 1930s, Jones was a leading political figure who established the Carver Democratic Club. He would become a legend for his work as a political leader, and much of that work included helping to build and develop the political careers of others.

Among those whom Jones helped support during their careers are former New York City mayor David Dinkins, Congressman Charlie Rangel and former lieutenant governor of New York and secretary of state for New York Basil Paterson. These three men, along with Percy Sutton, a politician and business leader, would eventually become known as Harlem's legendary political powerhouse, the "Gang of Four." Paterson's son David went on to become the first African American governor of the state of New York. David Paterson served in several political offices before he was sworn into the governor's office in March 2008. He served as lieutenant governor under former New York governor Eliot Spitzer, who resigned because of a prostitution scandal. Paterson endured his own political bruising for two years before ultimately deciding in 2010 not to seek the office again.

The People of Harlem

In East Harlem, as the population of Puerto Ricans and Italians grew, so did political activism. The work Adam Clayton Powell Jr. did on the west side, Oscar Garcia Rivera did on the east side. Rivera graduated from Columbia with an undergraduate degree and earned his law degree at St. John's College in 1930. It would not take long before he put his law degree to work. Over the years, Rivera worked in Puerto Rican communities on issues such as labor reform, voter registration and educational programs. In 1937, backed by the American Labor Party, the Republican Party and the City Fusion Party, Rivera defeated Tammany Hall and was elected a state assemblyman. Rivera's election made him the first Puerto Rican ever to be elected to public office within the continental United States.

Politics would become as vibrant a part of the East Harlem community as they were in West Harlem. While the Hotel Theresa served as an unofficial base for politicians, activists and entertainers on the west side, East Harlem had its own place that served as a political center.

From 1923 to 1933, Fiorello H. La Guardia represented East Harlem in the United States Congress. Prior to that, La Guardia was first elected to Congress in 1916, defeating Tammany Hall to represent a district in lower Manhattan. The 1916 election made La Guardia the first Italian American elected to Congress. As his popularity continued, at one point while he served the East Harlem community, La Guardia named the intersection of 116th Street and Lexington Avenue "Lucky Corner." It would be here that La Guardia would hold rallies on the eve of any of his elections.

In a move not often seen in politics, following his second term in Congress, La Guardia turned to city politics and was elected mayor of New York City in 1933. Popular among the people, La Guardia would pave the wave for other politicians such as Vito Marcantonio.

On December 2, 1939, La Guardia and his family watched as the first plane landed at the airport named in his honor—La Guardia Airport—which still bears his name today. La Guardia had been a big advocate of establishing a major airport in New York City. It seems quite unbelievable to think of it now, but until as late as the 1930s, New York City did not have a major airport of its own. In the 1920s, a small airport was built at North Beach, but it could not accommodate big planes and heavy volume. At the time, anyone traveling to New York City by plane would have to fly to New Jersey airports and then travel by other means into New York City. This, ironically, is still done today, with many travelers flying into Newark International Airport and then on to New York City. Today, this route is taken by choice. Prior to the 1920s, however, for New York City–bound travelers, there was no option but to stop in New Jersey.

La Guardia can in some ways be considered one of the first great champions of tourism to New York City. He believed that many people would flock to the city if transportation was easily accessible. He worked hard to get city and federal officials to give New York City money to build an airport. In fact, in a well-publicized publicity stunt, La Guardia took a flight to Chicago, and on the return to Newark Airport, he refused to exit, making the point that his ticket said "Chicago to New York." He did this surrounded by a ton of media representatives who subsequently rushed to report it in their newspapers.

Interestingly, La Guardia, who lived in Harlem, which is known for its arts and culture, would also leave his mark on the city of New York in the area of the arts. It was La Guardia, along with former city council president Newbold Morris, who pushed to create Manhattan's first performing arts center, a 2,750-seat facility that would become home to some of New York's best theater, music and dance.

A building constructed in 1923 as a meeting hall for members of the Ancient Order of the Nobles of the Mystic Shrine eventually became a city-owned property. That's when LaGuardia and Morris stepped in and saved the building from being destroyed and created Manhattan's first performing arts center. The City Center had its official opening on December 11, 1943, with a special performance by the New York Philharmonic. At this performance, Fiorello La Guardia took the helm as conductor of the orchestra, leading them in playing the national anthem. Eventually, the New York City Opera and the New York City Ballet were created at City Center before moving to Lincoln Center. Today, the New York City Center is home to a number of dance companies, including the Alvin Ailey American Dance Theater, whose dancers include a number who have studied at the Dance Theater of Harlem. And today, the Fiorello La Guardia Society exists at the City Center, working to keep the center and New York City thriving with vibrant new arts programming.

Politics and political activism in Harlem have often swayed between "street preachers" and officially ordained preachers to lawyers and elected politicians to those activists who stand up for the community when duty calls. Many of the latter have worked tirelessly within various organizations serving the Harlem community. Today, the torch of black political activism has largely been picked up by the National Action Network (NAN),[63] which is led by political activist and former Democratic presidential candidate

The People of Harlem

Million Man March supporters in Harlem. *Photo by Jamel Shabazz.*

Reverend Al Sharpton. The office, located on 145th Street in Harlem, is the national headquarters for the organization, which continues to fight civil rights and equality issues through rallies and other actions reminiscent of those taken in the 1950s and 1960s.

Sharpton, who serves as the president of NAN, is also the co-founder of the Education Equality Project, which, according to a NAN flyer promoting a rally, "is a leading civil rights movement to eliminate the racial and ethnic achievement gap in public education by working to create an effective school for <u>every child</u>." On the fifty-fifth anniversary of *Brown v. Board of Education* in May 2009, NAN led a "Close the Gap Rally" in Washington, D.C., with free bus transportation to and from the rally.

In the summer of 2011, Sharpton broke new ground by getting his own television show on the MSNBC television network. The 6:00 p.m. daily show is groundbreaking in the sense that, unlike most journalists who have to maintain strict separation between their personal activities and their work, Sharpton is able to continue his activism while he also hosts his own TV show.

A lesser-known figure in the history of New York politics is Hulan Edwin Jack Sr., a native of St. Lucia in the British West Indies. Early in his career, he achieved success both locally and nationwide, but he would fall in disgrace by the end of his career.

Hulan Jack entered New York politics in the 1930s, and in 1940, he was elected to represent Harlem in the state assembly. He resigned from the state assembly after he was elected Manhattan borough president in 1953. He was the first black borough president in New York City and the highest-ranking black elected official in the country during the 1950s.[64]

Jack was reelected as borough president in 1957, only to resign near the end of his term in 1960 after allegations that he had accepted an illegal gift worth $4,500. Many of his supporters accused government officials of racial discrimination. The setback, however, did not stop Jack, who would show that he had three political "lives." In 1968, he went back into politics and won election to the state assembly once again. He served one term before being convicted in 1970 by the federal government of conspiracy and conflict of interest. Jack was accused of "using improper means to promote certain products at groceries in Harlem."[65] Near the end of his life, Jack served as a political consultant to the conspiracy theorist Lyndon H. LaRouche Jr. Jack died in New York on December 19, 1986.

The 1950s and '60s were volatile and nation-changing decades for the United States of America. Prior to this time, different parts of the country had been operating under seemingly different laws. Jim Crow and segregation dominated the American South, while up north, they practiced their own brand of separation and exclusion. This was crystal clear to Harlemites even in the midst of the days of big bands, showgirls and superstars. For the average citizen, the glitz and glamour of Harlem nightlife was something they watched from a distance.

A number of presidential leaders have stopped in Harlem at the legendary corner of 125th Street and Seventh Avenue and the Hotel Theresa. In 1960, Harlem got a surprise visit from Cuba's Fidel Castro. After he arrived in New York City and set up at another hotel, a dispute ensued between Fidel Castro's entourage and the staff of a downtown hotel, and Castro and his crew moved uptown to the Hotel Theresa. At the time, America was in the midst of the black power movement, and the message of Communism at the time was attracting a number of African Americans. Castro received an overwhelming response when he appeared and addressed a massive crowd in Harlem. Castro again visited Harlem in 1995 and 2000, when he addressed the congregations at both Abyssinian Baptist Church and Riverside Church.

Inasmuch as Harlem has been a breeding ground for African Americans in the arts, it has been a breeding ground for those in politics as well. Perhaps few exemplify this more than the late Ronald Harmon Brown. Brown grew up in Harlem, and due to his father's work, he grew up in the center of Harlem's happenings. For several years in the late 1940s, his father, William "Bill" Harmon Brown, was the manager for the famed Hotel Theresa. The

The People of Harlem

Brown family lived in the hotel, and this is where young Ron Brown, a future secretary of commerce, would spend his Harlem childhood.

Ronald Harmon Brown was born on August 1, 1941, in Washington, D.C. His parents, Bill Brown and Gloria Osborne, met while students at Howard University, and in 1940, the couple married. Bill Brown had begun working for a federal housing agency, which took him and his family to Boston for a few years before he landed in New York. His experience in housing led to him being offered the top position at the Hotel Theresa. In part, the senior Brown can be credited with heightening the hotel's profile, making it a premier location for Harlem's elite.

Living at the Hotel Theresa put the Browns—and the young Brown in particular—right in the middle of Harlem's action. For Ron Brown, this set the stage for what would become his life of mixing and mingling in the political world and making things happen. Although he did not serve in an elected office, Ron Brown knew politics. And he knew politics so well that he grew up to become one of several people with Harlem roots who would make it to the White House. He served as secretary of commerce under President Bill Clinton. Brown died in 1996 in a plane crash in Croatia. At the time, he was leading a group of CEOs to that country to explore business opportunities in the region.

Former President Bill Clinton caused a stir when he announced several years ago that he would be moving his foundation's offices to Harlem. Some thought it was a publicity stunt, and others were simply skeptical and wondering if it was in some way going to negatively affect the Harlem community. But that criticism did not last long, and Harlem welcomed Clinton with a massive celebration and much anticipation. Today, the offices for the William J. Clinton Foundation[66] remain at 55 West 125th Street in Harlem. After he left office, President Clinton wanted his foundation to work on areas where he could make the most difference as a private citizen. Now, the organization has about 1,100 staff personnel and volunteers and offices in forty countries. The programs and partnerships that the Clinton Foundation is working on include health security; economic empowerment; leadership development and citizen service; and racial, ethnic and religious reconciliation.

In recent years, along with Reverend Al Sharpton, politically some of the most visible faces of politics with a Harlem connection have been Colin Powell and Congressman Charles Rangel. Powell, the son of Jamaican immigrants, was born on April 5, 1937, in Harlem. Until he was six years old, his family lived in Harlem before moving to the Bronx and later settling in Queens. Powell had a career in the military and was an army general and head of the Joint Chiefs of Staff before eventually serving as secretary of state under President George W. Bush.

Today, Harlem is represented in New York City Council by longtime representative Inez E. Dickens and in Congress by Congressman Charles Rangel, who has served the Harlem community for over forty years. A diligent soldier for the Harlem community, in recent years, Rangel was embroiled in controversy surrounding some of his real estate and business dealings. In March 2010, he resigned from his position as the chairman of the powerful Ways and Means Committee because of the controversy. Representative Rangel first joined Congress in 1970 after defeating the legendary Adam Clayton Powell Jr. While in office, Rangel became the first African American chairman of the Ways and Means Committee.

Rangel is one-fourth of the famed Harlem foursome the Gang of Four, which included Rangel, the late Percy Sutton, former New York deputy mayor Basil Paterson and former New York City mayor David Dinkins. Basil Paterson is the father of former New York governor David Paterson, who had been embroiled in his own political controversies. In March 2010, calls for Governor David Paterson's ouster came following a domestic violence incident involving one of his top aides. Paterson has been accused of contacting the alleged victim in the case and having several of his staff members also contact the woman in an effort to downplay the alleged attack. This incident, along with a number of bungled incidents throughout his term involving state matters, led to calls for Paterson's resignation. Like Governor Paterson, Charlie Rangel weathered his own political storms surrounding his office's use of funds and spending. Rangel, who has served Harlem in Congress for several decades, stood firm, defiantly stating that he would not leave office. Rangel is still serving at this time.

Any talk about Harlem's African American politics and history is remiss without talking about the legendary Percy Ellis Sutton. Sutton's personal story is remarkable and inspiring. In many ways, his approach to life and his amazing success and achievements represent what Harlem is all about—staying positive, persevering, believing and achieving.

At the tender age of twelve, as the youngest of fifteen children, Sutton stowed away on a train from Texas and headed to Harlem, New York. This act alone would serve as a peek into the determination and drive of Percy E. Sutton. Perhaps some of that determination came from the fact that his father was a former slave.

Sutton's professional accomplishments are astounding. A veteran of the Second World War, he served with the famous Tuskegee Airmen, earning two combat stars in two military theaters. The Tuskegee Airmen were the renowned black airmen who flew more than 1,500 combat missions at a time when the notion of black men being pilots was considered unthinkable. After his military service, he returned to New York, where amazingly, he worked two jobs—one at the post office and the other as a subway conductor—while attending Brooklyn Law School. As a civil rights lawyer, he later opened a law office in Harlem, serving the people of the community and eventually representing none other than Malcolm X.

Sutton then launched a political career in New York, ultimately earning a state assemblyman seat. He later was elected Manhattan borough president and, in 1977, unsuccessfully ran for mayor of New York City. Sutton would serve as a mentor, advisor and trailblazer to a number of African American leaders who followed in his footsteps. Those included former presidential candidate Jesse Jackson, whom Sutton advised during his two presidential runs; Congressman Charlie Rangel, former chairman of the powerful House Ways and Means Committee; former New York City mayor David Dinkins, the city's first African American mayor; and Basil Paterson, the former deputy mayor in New York City who would later see his own son, David, become governor of New York.

Percy Sutton's professional accomplishments are enormous, but it is what he did for others that made him the revered person that he was in Harlem and beyond. Governor Paterson said that Sutton was "a fiercely loyal, compassionate and truly kind soul" and "one of New York's and this nation's most influential African-American leaders." President Barack Obama called Sutton "a true hero" and said his "lifelong dedication to the fight for civil rights and his career as an entrepreneur and public servant made the rise of countless young African-Americans possible."[67]

Throughout his life and career, he merged his commitment to public service with his business acumen. When the famous Apollo Theater was at risk of being torn down, Sutton headed a group that saved it. In the early '70s, with his brother Oliver, Sutton purchased WLIB-AM, which became the first black-owned radio station in New York City. He would eventually become a media powerhouse, one of the first African Americans to own and operate a successful media company. At the time of his death in late 2009, from the outpouring from political officials and Harlem residents, it became clear that Sutton's lasting impact was his role as mentor and advisor to so many. Reverend Al Sharpton said, "When there was a crisis, you could always call him for counsel and support…I don't know what we'll do without his guiding hand."[68]

In 2007, the Honorable Percy E. Sutton Way was named in Harlem. From 124th Street up to 142nd Street along Fifth Avenue was renamed to honor the businessman and civil rights leader. When Sutton died in December 2009, New York mayor Michael Bloomberg honored him by ordering all city flags to be flown at half staff.

While much attention was focused on the men who were making moves in politics and business, not much was said about the women. Nevertheless, women were just as politically active in communities and organizations. One woman in particular worked tirelessly for her entire life on behalf of equal rights for all women, particularly African American women.

Dorothy Irene Height never held a political office; however, she worked tirelessly throughout her lifetime for the rights of all women. Known for her love of hats, Height was a champion of civil rights and social justice and is widely recognized as the only woman who is considered part of the civil rights "Big Six," which includes Dr. Martin Luther King Jr., Whitney Young, James Farmer, John Lewis, A. Philip Randolph and Roy Wilkins.

Although Height was always working together with the "Big Six" during the civil rights era, women were often not given prominent positions. In an April 2010 *New York Times* article about Height, the newspaper calls her an "unsung giant of the civil rights era." The article goes on to say:

> *Over the years, historians have made much of the so-called "Big Six" who led the civil rights movement: the Rev. Dr. Martin Luther King Jr., James Farmer, John Lewis, A. Philip Randolph, Roy Wilkins and Whitney M. Young Jr. Ms. Height, the only woman to work regularly alongside them on projects of national significance, was very much the unheralded seventh, the leader who was cropped out, figuratively and often literally, of images of the era.*

Accomplished in her own right, Height earned bachelor's and master's degrees in psychology from New York University. She would garner a long résumé of work in the social justice arena but perhaps is best known for her work with two organizations, the YWCA and the National Council of Negro Women (NCNW). She spent approximately about forty years with each group. Height lived in Harlem in the 1930s in the midst of Harlem's Renaissance and at one time was the assistant executive director of the Harlem YWCA.

FOODS AND FLAVORS OF HARLEM

With so many people from around the world now calling Harlem home, that touch of "home" that comes with a hearty meal can come from anywhere in the world—and it can be found in Harlem. It has long been believed that in New York City, if you want a taste of soul food, you have to head uptown. Soul food is definitely still in Harlem, but nowadays, it may be just a few blocks down the street from a steakhouse, a French café or a wine bar.

For years, SYLVIA'S RESTAURANT (328 Lenox Avenue, 212.996.0660) has been the place most people have sought out to get some down-home cooking in Harlem. For more than thirty years, Sylvia Woods's restaurant has been soothing the palates of visitors and hometown folks alike. Ms. Woods has also passed the baton to her niece, who owns MELBA'S (300 West 114th Street, 212.864.7777, www.melbasrestaurant.com).

Known for its benevolent portions, AMY RUTH'S (113 West 116th Street, 212.280.8779) soul food is so scrumptious and plentiful it has guests waiting in line to dine. Once inside, guests can view photos and other items highlighting the visits of famous entertainers and politicians and their meal choices. For those looking for a buffet meal, MANNA'S (54 East 125th Street, 212.360.4975, www.soulfood.com) has been serving up soul food by the pound for years. Manna's has been a favorite of locals, who go there to grab a quick bite of soul food to sit down and eat or to take home.

One of newest restaurants offering soul food is Jacob Restaurant (www.jacobrestaurant.com), which offers southern-style, Caribbean and continental cuisine in a buffet setting. In just a few years since its opening, Jacob Restaurant is growing and has several locations in Harlem.

At the top of Central Park North, MISS MAMIE'S SPOONBREAD TOO (366 West 110th Street, 212.865.6744, www.spoonbreadinc.com) serves you soul food in a setting reminiscent of your grandmother's kitchen. Owner Norma Jean Darden and her sister Carole have coauthored a bestselling cookbook, *Spoonbread and Strawberry Wine*. Both Miss Mamie's and MISS MAUDE'S SPOONBREAD (547 Lenox Avenue, 212.690.3100) serve big portions that make you feel right at home.

While Harlem and soul food at one time may have been synonymous, today one can find eateries featuring flavors from around the world. Whether it is Caribbean, Latin American, French or Italian cuisine, you can find it in Harlem. A Cajun/Creole restaurant brings the French Quarter to Harlem. The CREOLE JAZZ AND SUPPER CLUB (2167 Third Avenue, 212.876.8838, www.creolenyc.com) brings a little bit of Louisiana uptown.

Flavors from many places in the Caribbean offer traditional foods from Puerto Rico, the Dominican Republic and Cuba. Yvette Seda, the postal worker who grew up spending time with family in East Harlem, says food was a big part of those family gatherings for many Puerto Ricans.

"We do rice and *gandulas*. That's rice with pigeon peas. I think it's from Puerto Rico. That is our really typical food, *arroz con gandulas*," Seda says. She recalls several Puerto Rican dishes that are staples that she remembers from family gatherings and social outings.

"One of our favorite dishes for the holidays—people make it because it's a lot of work—is *pasteles*. *Pasteles*, that's a lot of work there. It looks like tamales. It's a wrap," she says while explaining the extensive work involved in preparing the dish.

> *Plantains, you grate it. You have that on the side and then you make like pork, the meat and you make it with sauce and potatoes on the side and then you take*

The site of the popular former M&G Soul Food Restaurant. The diner-style twenty-four-hour restaurant closed unexpectedly sometime between 2008 and 2009.

Foods and Flavors of Harlem

The Cotton Club.

> *a plantain leaf and you put it there and scoop some meat with potatoes and sauce. Then you wrap it and you seal it, tie it and you boil it. It's delicious, but it's a lot of work. We usually do this, but we do it on the holidays, but that's a typical food. Besides* arroz con gandulas, *it's pasteles.*

FLORIDITA (3219 Broadway, 212.662.0090) offers affordable Spanish food in a diner setting.

Just a few blocks away is perhaps one of the most obviously transformed areas in Harlem when you consider the number of new eating establishments in the area, as well as improvements to the general landscape.

The community surrounding Twelfth Avenue and 125th Street up through 135th Street has seen a complete transformation. Buildings that were empty are now housing trendy restaurants. One of the most well-known entertainment establishments that has been in this area in recent years is Harlem's legendary Cotton Club (656 West 125th Street, 212.663.7980, www.cottonclub-newyork.com). Although the current location is not the original site of the famous club, visitors still flock to the Cotton Club for a night of food, fun, entertainment and nostalgia.

Harlem is developing very quickly, and with this comes a wealth of new restaurants and cafés throughout the community. Anyone wishing to observe a little of the cultural history of Harlem, along with the foods from various cultures, may want to check out Taste Harlem Food and Cultural Tours (www.tasteharlem.com), which provides a combination tour of particular aspects of Harlem along with some of the different cuisines that are available.

CULTURAL CRUSADES
FROM JAZZ TO HIP-HOP

Art in Harlem is virtually inseparable from the worldwide arts community. Foray into practically any area of the arts and Harlem has surely put its stamp on it. From writers, poets and visual artists to singers, dancers, theater, jazz and hip-hop, the arts and Harlem are practically synonymous.

The cultural presence in Harlem can be seen and felt everywhere you look. In galleries and cultural arts organizations and museums or historic landmarks, wherever you are in Harlem, you are close to the arts and culture. Ever since the Harlem Renaissance of the 1920s and 1930s, the neighborhood has been an inspiration for artists. Today, countless artists use Harlem as a backdrop in fictional stories, as a setting in a film or as a theme or song title in many genres of music.

R&B singer Alicia Keys used a well-known Harlem eatery as the setting for the music video for her popular song "You Don't Know My Name." She also named one of her songs "Harlem Nocturne," which is on her *The Diary of Alicia Keys* CD. Jazz great Duke Ellington named one of his songs "Take the 'A' Train," which is a reference to one of the longest subway train routes running through New York, including Harlem.

The Harlem Arts Alliance, a collective of nearly four hundred individual artists and arts organizations, each year sponsors ArtCrawl Harlem (www.artcrawlharlem.com), a guided trolley bus tour of a variety of Harlem art galleries. Averlyn Archer is a co-founder of ArtCrawl Harlem and owner and gallery director of Canvas Paper and Stone Art Gallery (Striver's Row, 2611 Frederick Douglass Blvd., Studio 2N, between West 139th and West 140th Streets, 212.694.1747, www.canvaspaperandstone.com), one of the galleries on the artcrawl tour. In 2009, other galleries on the tour included the Essie Green Galleries, Gallery One (aka Donna Dove), Heath Gallery, Indigo Arms Guest House Gallery, Simmons Gallery and the Rio II Gallery.

Archer, who is a lawyer, went to City College and has been in Harlem for twenty years. Staunchly committed to the arts scene and the Harlem arts community, she says, "I love art. I think it's important. I think it feeds us." She previously owned the American Vision 145 gallery in Harlem but had to move to a new location. Her Canvas Paper and Stone Gallery, a contemporary fine art gallery, opened in January 2007, and her first show, entitled "Just a Little Bit," featured several artists and opened in February 2007. Since then, she has been very active in the Harlem arts community, working with various arts organizations to promote the arts.

In addition to being one of the lead galleries for Harlem's annual arts crawl, Archer's gallery helped celebrate the recent reopening of El Museo del Barrio (1230 Fifth Avenue at 104th Street, 212.831.7272, www.elmuseo.org), a leading museum and cultural center highlighting the work of Puerto Rican and Latin American artists from around the world. The celebration included a tour of East Harlem galleries, including My Arte Gallery, Poet's Den Gallery, Media Noche, TAFA Studios and Taller Boricua.

El Museo del Barrio hosted a big celebration of its own upon its reopening in October 2009 after being closed for a year and a half. Located on "Museum Mile," El Museo recently celebrated its forty-year anniversary. The museum, which is located in a building that used to be an orphanage, was founded by artists and has been on Museum Mile since 1977. The reopening included a weekend of family activities including music, storytelling, dance and comedy performances. Part of the goal of renovating the building was to make it more inviting for visitors. This includes additional areas for public events. The café, courtyard and rooftop can all accommodate performances, as can the theater, which in the past has hosted mayoral debates. Once one finishes their museum visit, there are a number of East Harlem lounges and bars they can enjoy, many of which have opened in recent years.

The Harlem Arts Alliance (www.harlemaa.org) provides advocacy and support for both artists and the arts in Harlem. It is one of the only organizations of its kind in the area. The group offers a number of programs designed to help artists fund and promote their work. One of its signature programs, Arts, Rootz and Rhythm, provides free public presentations showcasing Harlem artists. Each October, the group sponsors Arts Advocacy in Harlem, an annual series of seminars, panel discussions and events held in various Harlem venues with an aim to promote the importance of the arts in the Harlem community.

The tradition of the arts in Harlem extends well beyond jazz and the Harlem Renaissance. Particularly, the theater arts have had a long history in Harlem. From burlesque to acting troupes to singers and dancers, the performing arts have always thrived in Harlem. Theaters such as the Lafayette Theater, the legendary Apollo Theater and the National Black Theatre (2031–33 125th Street and Fifth Avenue, www.nationalblacktheatre.org) host a variety of performances, from plays to film screenings. Officially known as the National Black Theatre Institute of Action Arts, it was founded by Dr. Barbara Ann Teer with the goal of operating from "an African context of a spirit culture." In 2009, the theater hosted the Queer Black Cinema Film Festival (www.queerblackcinema.org), which is led by Angel Brown, who works with filmmakers to help give their work featuring gay and lesbian themes broader exposure. Brown says that the National Black Theatre is now her organization's home and the community can expect much more in the future.

In December 2009, Brown's company hosted a second screening of a popular film by writer and director Faith Trimel. Trimel's film, *Family*, is about a group of African American women who are lesbians who make a pact that within thirty days they will all come out to their families. They do this but must struggle with issues including homophobia, hate crimes, religion and more that are particularly difficult within African American communities. The film is excellent, and the packed audience's response to the film was overwhelmingly positive, with laughter, clapping, sighs and cheers throughout the film.

There are many acclaimed schools and arts organizations throughout Harlem, such as the Harlem School of the Arts (645 Saint Nicholas Avenue, 212.926.4100, www.harlemschoolofthearts.org), the world-famous Boys Choir of Harlem (www.boyschoirofharlem.org) and the renowned Dance Theatre of Harlem (www.dancetheatreofharlem.org).

Art can be seen virtually anywhere in Harlem—in museums, in offices, in retail stores and even on some security gates that protect some of Harlem's shops from potential bandits. For instance, if you stroll along 125th after the shops have closed, you will see numerous gates covered with murals and other colorful artwork, much of it produced by well-known local and international artist Franco the Great (www.francothegreat.com).

Franco the Great's work appears in churches, restaurants, nightclubs, nursery schools, children's rooms and more. One of his works appears at New York's Port Authority station at 42nd Street. But in Harlem, Franco the Great is famous for his productions that can be seen on the security gates of numerous businesses throughout Harlem. In the community, he is known as the "Picasso of Harlem," and some refer to Harlem's 125th Street as "Franco's Boulevard." However, New York City Council has moved to ban all retail stores from using the gray gates that have served as a canvas for Franco the Great and many others, which will mean that these artists will lose a platform. New York City Council voted that in the coming years, all installed security gates for retailers would need to be mesh or grille-style gates, and after 2026, all gates will have to be mesh style or see-through. Until then, Franco the Great will keep creating, and his gate works will live on, adding beauty and vibrancy to Harlem's 125th Street.

Jazz

Jazz and Harlem are virtually synonymous. In the 1920s, and 1930s, numerous jazz musicians who would later become canons of the jazz era moved to or were newly settled in New York City. Without a doubt, the swing era of jazz was the most exciting and electrifying time of the jazz movement. As musicians from all over the country made their way to Harlem, they would establish themselves as future legends—Ella Fitzgerald, Chick Webb, Count Basie, Duke Ellington, Fletcher Henderson, Sarah Vaughan, Billy Eckstine and countless others. Collectively, they were the "change agents" for jazz music. As singers and musicians of the swing era, they forever changed how jazz music would be played.

Swing music and dancing became a huge phenomenon, almost a national obsession, taking jazz to heights of popularity never achieved before or since. More jazz musicians gained favor with the general public, more audiences turned to jazz as a backdrop for dancing and entertainment, than at any other time in history. Never before had jazz so dominated the field of popular music.[69]

Jazz master Duke Ellington lived and worked in Harlem when Harlem was in swing.

Dances such as the Grizzly Bear, the Mooche, the Slow Drag, the Black Bottom, the Shimmy and the Charleston, among others, took off and dominated the club scene. One of the most famous dances of the swing era—the Lindy Hop—likely started in a Harlem nightclub. The most spectacular and exciting dance step of the swing era, the fast, furious Lindy Hop burst forth in 1928, probably from the Savoy Ballroom. It was developed there in the 1930s and taken to exceptional heights, literally and figuratively. The dance, encompassing a tension between partnering and individual expression, featured improvised breakaways and athletic aerial movements or "air" steps—pioneered by the Harlem dancer Frankie Manning—in which women were tossed into the air like rag dolls. As the Lindy Hop caught on, energetic young dancers expanded its routine of floor and aerial steps at ballrooms and competitions. Known in white communities as the Jitterbug, the step drew young enthusiasts across America. Twirling dancers, swirling skirts, exuberant smiles, youthful energy, virtuosic displays, the night charged with excitement—this was the Lindy Hop.[70] These dances were done at clubs such as the world-renowned Savoy Ballroom and the world-famous Cotton Club, among many others.

Dancing like this at the Savoy Ballroom is what made Harlem the place to be.

Above: The Lenox Lounge is a Harlem jazz stalwart that is still thriving today.

Right: The *New York Amsterdam News*'s 1929 "Battle of Jazz" newspaper article. Bands from the North and South competed in this first-of-its-kind event.

Southern Orchestras to Engage in 'Battle of Jazz'

The Savoy Ballroom on Wednesday night, May 8, is again about to do the unusual and is leading the way for the first intersectional battle of jazz music ever held between the South and the North, in which six of the country's leading orchestras will vie for musical honors.

For this "Battle of Jazz" the Savoy, at a tremendous cost, is bringing to this city three of the South's best orchestras, Ike Dixon from Baltimore and Johnson's Happy Pals from Richmond, Va. These two orchestras, in conjunction with the Missourians, acknowledged sensations, will defend the southern laurels, and if advance information means anything they are coming well prepared for this battle, and are ready to blow their last note in the claim that they are the better orchestras.

The North, however, is ready for this southern invasion and has lined up three of this city's best orchestras for the defense and feels confident that they will both outplay and outstomp the boys from the South.

Fess Williams and his Royal Flush Orchestra, Charlie Johnson and his Small's Paradise Orchestra, and Duke Ellington and his Cotton Club Orchestra are ready to do or die in the defense of their city, and have their musical bars in readiness with which to smite.

All in all, Wednesday night, May 8, will provide an evening of exceptional entertainment for all music lovers and everybody is anxiously awaiting this glorious "Battle of Jaz" between the South and the North.

Harlem had many extremely popular clubs during this era—Minton's Playhouse, the Lenox Lounge and many others—but the Savoy and the Cotton Club were the biggest and most popular. Eventually, these two clubs, which were always jam packed with dancers, came to symbolize Harlem and the era. The Savoy Ballroom opened its doors on March 12, 1926, on Lenox Avenue between 140th and 141st Streets.

Harlem's famous Cotton Club at one time during its early years was part owned by notorious boxing champion Jack Johnson, whose confidence, style and lack of fear were rarely displayed by black men during his era. This made Johnson a legendary figure. Unafraid of the status quo and committed to living life on his own terms, Johnson was fiercely determined—in the ring and outside of it. His co-ownership of the Cotton Club was brief, but Johnson, like other sports and entertainment figures, had Harlem as his playground.

Nearly all the jazz greats and other entertainers of the era at one time or another made their way to Harlem. Most of the neighborhood clubs were close together, which added to the overall sense of community in the jazz world.

Hip-Hop

In 1979, Harlem's Kurtis Blow (Curtis Walker) became the first rapper to sign a contract with a major record company.[71] There would be others who would also make their mark in the genre who had "Harlem roots."

Mason "Ma$e" Betha became extraordinarily successful during the late '90s with his 1997 CD release *Harlem World*. Born in Jacksonville, Florida, he grew up in Harlem. Signed to Sean "Puffy" Combs's Bad Boy record label, Ma$e was unstoppable and on top of the hip-hop music scene, with constant radio spins and video airplays. Known for his affinity for "bling," Ma$e was known for celebrating the excesses of success—gold, jewelry, expensive cars, expensive clothes and all that money could buy. Even his moniker—Ma$e—when written out was printed with a dollar sign replacing the "s." But Ma$e shocked the hip-hop world a couple of years later, after his 1999 CD release, when he announced that he was leaving hip-hop to become a minister. Most who heard the news were shocked and surprised, especially rap music fans who had helped catapult him to the top. Others snickered and marveled at the notion of a former rapper entering the ministry.

What Ma$e was deciding to do had never been done before: a hip-hop star—and crossover success at that—on top of the music world bowing out.

A star with hit records, massive radio and video airplay, magazine covers and swooning girls quitting the game and finding religion. "Yeah, right" was the general response.

Now, more than ten years, a wife, two children, one church, a television program and two honorary degrees later, Mason Betha (www.masonbetha.org) has silenced his critics. In 2001, he started SANE (Saving a Nation Endangered) Church International, now El Elyon International Church. Plans are in store for a branch of the church in Phoenix, Arizona. And through his daily television program, *Born to Succeed*, he reaches millions of people across the nation.

Ma$e did eventually feel the pull of the music industry and, in 2004, made a third CD, *Welcome Back*, which became another chart topper for the rapper. The CD also was praised by music industry and well-known faith scholars for its thought-provoking lyrics with positive undertones.

Hip-hop itself is more than just music. Hip-hop is dance. It is deejays. It is clothes and style. And it is the media. Hip-hop magazines chronicle all the facets of the genre. Along with the words, there are the images.

Renowned Harlem-based photographer Johnny Nunez has been capturing the faces of hip-hop since 1997. The Harlem-based photographer's journey to becoming a photographer is an interesting and inspiring story about perseverance and faith. Nunez tells the story in his DVD, *Shooting Star(s), The Rise of Hip Hop Photographer Johnny Nunez*, which was released in 2009.

Adopted as a baby by a Puerto Rican family in Brooklyn, Johnny battled racism and ridicule as a kid because he was a black kid in a Latino family. Later in life, while he was in school studying radiology, he was kicked out. This initiated a downward spiral in his life until he nearly lost everything and had to start delivering pizzas. In his DVD, he describes how humiliating it was for him to be delivering pizzas and eventually having to deliver to a friend of his who questioned what he was doing. After fudging an answer about needing money to pay some bills, he continues to talk about how painful it was for him to accept the dollar tip and how he screamed and banged on his car horn in frustration after making that delivery.

Johnny Nunez's life took a huge turn once he was given a camera by a friend. That move would turn out to be life changing for Nunez, who is today one of the most sought-after hip-hop industry photographers. He has snapped photographs of Jay Z, Kanye West, Russell Simmons and numerous others. In fact, his long business relationship with Russell Simmons led to an invitation for Nunez to work on a marketing campaign that would take them to London, Dubai and Paris.

Nunez, like early renowned Harlem-based photographers Gordon Parks and James Van Der Zee, is capturing the era he is living in—the hip-hop era—with his camera lenses. He is following in their tradition, as well as the tradition of Morgan and Marvin Smith, twin brother photographers who are often overlooked but who in fact influenced Parks himself. The brothers arrived in Harlem from Kentucky near the beginning of the Great Depression and began capturing images of Harlem in the post-Renaissance years. Just as Nunez and other photographers are taking photos documenting hip-hop today, Van Der Zee, the Smith brothers and Gordon Parks documented yesteryear and Harlem life in general.

As Nunez captures hip-hop through his lenses, an individual's naked eye can see hip-hop all day long in Harlem. More than just music, hip-hop is a culture. Wherever you are in Harlem, one can see elements of hip-hop, especially when it comes to styles and dress. Much to the chagrin of some people, the baggy jean style for men began in hip-hop and now has spread throughout mainstream culture. Baggy jeans, a big T-shirt or polo and the latest "kicks" or sneakers is the unofficial uniform of a hip-hop man. For women, there has never really been one specific kind of uniform, just sort of a "keep up with the current fashion" approach.

To really learn the history of hip-hop in the city where it was born, check out Hush Tours (www.zerve.com//hiphoplook/walk), which offers a Harlem Hip Hop Walking Tour. Guided by hip-hop historians, participants visit places such as the legendary Apollo Theater, which has hosted some popular contests and competitions in the past, and numerous Harlem clubs and other locations that are part of the hip-hop scene.

Three brothers in Harlem.
Photo by Jamel Shabazz.

FAITH AND RELIGION IN THE COMMUNITY

Just as Harlem is known for the Harlem Renaissance, it is also known for its historic churches and houses of worship. Over the years, through wars, the Great Depression and the civil rights movement, African Americans have stood strong in their faith to see them through. As they migrated to Harlem from the American South, the tradition of going to church and standing on faith never left them.

Although large numbers of African Americans moved to Harlem during the early twentieth century, prior to their arrival, Jews and Italians lived in the community, and they, too, practiced their faith. In East Harlem, Spanish immigrants also maintained a strong faith and church.

Today, visitors can go uptown to Harlem and experience one of these African American church services for themselves, which are known for vibrant singing and lively preaching. Companies such as Harlem Spirituals Gospel & Jazz Tours (212.391.0900, www.harlemspirituals.com) provide tours in Harlem where guests visit a local church and eating establishment to get a "taste of Harlem."

From the eccentric street preacher to the fully trained and ordained ministers, Harlem has been home to all with a spiritual message. Houses of worship in Harlem are as diverse in denomination as the people who are attending, with names like Abyssinian Baptist Church (138th Street between Lenox and Adam Clayton Powell Boulevard); Harlem Church of Jesus Christ of Latter-Day Saints, Mormon (128th Street and Lenox Avenue); St. Philip's Protestant Episcopal Church (134th Street and Adam Clayton Powell Boulevard); Salem United Methodist Church (129th Street and Adam Clayton Powell Boulevard); United House of Prayer for All People (125th

Abyssinian Baptist Church.

Riverside Church.

Faith and Religion in the Community

Mother Zion AME Church.

Street and Frederick Douglass Boulevard); and Nation of Islam Mosque #7 (127th Street and Lenox Avenue), which at one time was led by Malcolm X.

James Weldon Johnson writes in *Black Manhattan*, "There are something like one hundred and sixty coloured churches in Harlem. A hundred of these could be closed and there would be left a sufficient number to supply the religious needs of the community." He also acknowledges the need for churches in a community like Harlem.

> *The multiplicity of churches in Harlem, and in every other Negro community, is commonly accounted for by the innate and deep religious emotion of the race. Conceding the strength and depth of this emotion, there is also the vital fact that coloured churches provide their members with a great deal of enjoyment, aside from the joys of religion. Indeed, a Negro church is for its members much more besides a place of worship. It is a social centre, it is a club, it is an arena for the exercise of one's*

Harlem in the Twentieth Century

Pilgrim Pentecostal Church, East Harlem.

capabilities and powers, a world in which one may achieve self-realization and preferment. Of course, a church means something of the same sort to all groups; but with the Negro all these attributes are magnified because of the fact that they are so curtailed for him in the world at large.[72]

Faith practiced in Harlem since the beginning of the twentieth century has been diverse in both the religions practiced as well as religious structures. Harlem houses of faith have run the gamut from small storefront churches to mega churches with congregations totaling in the thousands. These houses of worship include a variety of denominations such as Baptist, Methodist, Episcopal, Catholic and Presbyterian. There is no one dominant religion that is practiced in Harlem. In general, whatever one's faith, there is something for everybody.

TOURISTS AND TRANSITIONS

Visitors travel to Harlem daily and can be seen everywhere. Walking the sidewalks. In the stores. In restaurants and coffee shops. On the tour buses.

As the Apollo Theater remembered Michael Jackson just days after news of his death broke in June 2009, buses full of tourists pulled over and let the visitors step off the buses and take pictures of the impromptu remembrance that took place at the entrance to the theater. Men, women and children of all ages and nationalities gathered in front of the theater to share stories, sing and dance to MJ's tunes. They also signed the tribute wall abruptly constructed by Apollo Theater workers to give visitors and mourners a place to write their thoughts and share words of sympathy. This celebration, without condemnation of Michael Jackson's life, was once again a time when the people of Harlem showed what Harlem is about.

It had been over thirty years since Michael Jackson, with his brothers as the Jackson 5, stepped onto the famous stage and won the world-renowned amateur night contest. From there, of course, their illustrious career took off, and the rest, as they say, is history. But it was the people who voted on that particular night who came from Harlem and throughout the New York area who buoyed the group and sent them off to stratospheric heights. They helped launch the Jackson 5's music career, and on this day of mourning and celebration of Michael Jackson, they showed that Harlem never forgets.

While tourists make Harlem a regular stop nowadays, it was not always that way. Lora Bell, a maintenance worker who has lived in Harlem for many years, says the perception of Harlem and the economic state of the community in previous years contributed to a negative view of the area. "Harlem wasn't nothing. Harlem wasn't nothing at first. It wasn't respected. Harlem used to be this place to live where they just wanted to fight all the time."

Bell says that people used to snicker at one saying that they were from Harlem. But now, that has changed:

> *Now, everybody wants to say Harlem now because Harlem is built up. Like I'm proud where I live at now 'cause it's not that much drama, you know. I'm glad white people are moving to Harlem. It don't bother me 'cause I get along with anybody. Before I used to say "ill Harlem" 'cause Harlem wasn't sh*#...I mean nothing. I mean back in the '90s, it was real bad. It was like nothing was moving but drugs.*

But today, the perception of living in Harlem has a different meaning. With new development and new influxes of people, what once was perhaps a predominantly negative view is now most definitely looking up. After enduring the ups and downs that many urban communities will at some point face—overflowing immigration, residential overcrowding, crime, job loss and economic turbulence among its residents—Harlem continues to be a hot spot.

According to an April 2009 *AM New York* article about falling real estate prices in Manhattan, the median sales price of a home in Harlem in the fourth quarter of 2007 was $499,999. At the end of 2008, the median sales price was just slightly lower at $496,500. However, the median listing price was $725,000. Out of 715 listings, 304 homes, or 42 percent of the properties, recently had price cuts averaging just over 10 percent.

Attracted by some of Harlem's landmark institutions and the community's legendary reputation, tour companies are bringing thousands of tourists

The Bradhurst condominium building in Harlem is just one of many new condos in the area. The Canvas, Paper and Stone Art Gallery is located here.

Tourists and Transitions

to Harlem on a regular basis. In earlier days, the familiar double-decker tour buses that can be seen throughout Manhattan may have been viewed skeptically by some residents, but now they are fixtures in the community.

B&W Charters, Inc. (www.bwcharters.com), a Kalamazoo, Michigan-based bus touring company owned and operated by Gene Wright and Paul Best, has been giving Harlem tours for twenty-five years. Wright says, "Because of the history of Harlem and the stars, the Apollo and the Cotton Club," the company started doing the tours essentially from the time it started the business. Senior citizens, retirees and church groups are the main groups of people who have participated in the tours. Typically, Wright says, B&W Charters, Inc. hosts the tours three or four times per year, and the company does have a special Harlem itinerary. "Many famous people came from New York. Entertainers. Athletes. Congressmen. People should come and recognize that Harlem has deep roots as part of New York City," says Wright.

Tourists cruising through Harlem will undoubtedly quickly be swept up into the energy that flows through the area. Immediately, many tourists will wonder what is happening on the busy sidewalks below their double-decker bus seats. From their vantage point, some of the streets below can look chaotic. Street vendors line the sidewalks. Messengers and various promoters shout out their agendas and political causes. African immigrants speak to one another in their native languages. African women stand outside hair-braiding shops attempting to get new customers. Young people, dressed in their hip-hop-influenced clothing, laugh and joke among each other. Older folks walk with their peers or sit nearby, observing the surroundings.

There was a time when tourists did not visit Harlem like they do today. But that has definitely changed. For one, there are more tour companies offering

Harlem T-shirts for sale.

trips to the area. Some tour the general Harlem neighborhood, while others specialize in food, church and music tours. CitySights NY (212.812.2700, www.citysightsny.com) offers tours throughout New York City, including a special Harlem tour. Known for its churches and other religious facilities, the Harlem On Sunday tour (212.246.0597) lets visitors check out typical historical sites in the area, as well as attend a Harlem church service and eat a "traditional Soul food" meal or watch a Harlem gospel choir perform.

Les Forster, who has spent his whole life in Harlem, says that it is unfair to paint Harlem negatively and that those who express hesitancy in visiting the area are most likely visitors.

> *I think that's more tourists'* [view]. *I wouldn't say that's people who've been living in Harlem their whole life. Like I'm so used to Harlem. I think I can go to any block or any area in Harlem and feel comfortable because that's like my stomping* [ground]. *That's my backyard. So yeah, I definitely say that's more a tourist's view because it's not like that. I mean just like in every other place it's crime everywhere. I say by summertime, it's more fun in Harlem anyway. Like it's cookouts going on, block parties. So in my view, Harlem is still and always is going to be historic, monumental, like a good place to be. Even though at that time, it might have its bad times. But that's anywhere in the world. Harlem to L.A. to Nevada. Wherever you are. That could be anywhere.*

HARLEM RECREATION AND RELAXATION

With two riverfronts, the coasts of the Harlem community are ready made for fun and relaxation. And with the support of the City of New York and its efforts to keep residents of New York City moving while having fun and staying healthy, things like the citywide bike path are a welcome addition.

In 2006, the City of New York committed to a plan to expand its existing bike lanes and paths across all five boroughs. Buttressed by the Hudson River to the west and the Harlem River to the east, Harlem is located in north Manhattan, just above Central Park. If you started on the bike path in West Harlem, you could then essentially bike almost the entire island of Manhattan starting in West Harlem and ending in East Harlem.

Since 2006, New York City has expanded its bicycle lanes and routes by 200 miles. Throughout New York City, there are more than 620 lane miles of bike lanes, paths and routes. Within the last six years, the number of commuter cyclists in New York City has doubled. And in the last year alone, commuter cycling has increased by 35 percent in the city.[73] To accommodate these rising numbers, the Department of Transportation has installed more than five thousand newly designed sidewalk bicycle racks across the city. New, sleek bicycle parking shelters that provide indoor parking for bikes are also being installed.

The city's approach to bicycling has not gone unrecognized. *Bicycling Magazine* has named New York City one of the best big cities for cycling, and the League of American Bicyclists has awarded the Big Apple with the prestigious Bicycle Friendly Communities Award. The City of New York, the Department of Transportation, the Department of City Planning and the Department of Parks and Recreation have collaborated to produce the NYC Cycling Map, which is available for free to the public.

In Harlem on the west side, the bike path—which extends around the island of Manhattan—will take you past Riverbank State Park (679 Riverside Drive, 212.694.3600, www.nysparks.state.ny.us), which is home to an ice-skating rink, an indoor pool, a football field and outdoor track, all open to the public. A small fee is required to access the facilities. The park is near 145th Street in Harlem and is easily accessible by subway.

Farther uptown at 155th Street sits Rucker Park, the famous Harlem playground where legions of famous basketball players have graced the court. Every summer, the Rucker Basketball League hosts its popular basketball tournament.

Every year in August, the Harlem community celebrates Harlem Week with numerous cultural and informational events held throughout Harlem. Various events, ranging from museum activities and theater shows to jazz and other music performances, are held. Each September or early October, the festive and colorful annual African American parade kicks off with thousands of individuals, children and families lining Harlem's broad streets to watch.

In recent years, bowling has made a comeback as a social activity of choice. And if you are in Harlem, there's no need to head downtown. Harlem Lanes (2116 Adam Clayton Powell Boulevard, 212.678.BOWL (2695), www.harlemlanes.com), a sleek, cosmopolitan facility, is designed for more than just bowling. It is also able to host networking events and other social gatherings. Not just a bowling alley, this popular Harlem spot covers several floors in the building and has a bar to whet your palate and a deejay to keep you moving.

Going to the movies has never gone out of style and most likely never will. Former NBA star Earvin "Magic" Johnson apparently knew this when he decided to develop MJ Harlem 9 (2309 Frederick Douglass Boulevard and 125th Street), a movie theater complex that is part of the AMC theater group and shows major film releases. Once you enter the building, you immediately get the sense of culture and heritage that is so much a part of Harlem.

For starters, before you reach the theaters on the upper level, you must past the Harlem Hip Hop Culture Center (www.h2c2harlem.com). According to its website, the center is "dedicated to promoting success in youth through education and mentoring. The goal of the center is to become a bridge between youth and adults as well as the community at large."[74] With a quick peek inside their doors, one can see some of the exhibits and artifacts of hip-hop yesteryear on display. With an exhibit space of eight thousand square feet, there is plenty of room. Giant photos of people wearing the hip-hop styles of their eras—late '70s, the '80s and the '90s—hang on the walls. Glass enclosures display decorated sneakers, some of famous rappers. Some of the photos featured are the work of acclaimed New York photographer Jamel Shabazz, author of the popular photography collections *Back in the Days* and *A Time Before Crack*, both of which chronicle hip-hop in New York communities over the past few decades.

If one wants to simply relax and enjoy Harlem's parks, there are several options for that. The West Harlem Piers Park (near 125th Street and Broadway, www.nycgovparks.org) was once a parking lot in a neglected section of Harlem. With unoccupied buildings nearby and limited entertainment choices, for many years the area was a place to think about for its possibilities. After years of redevelopment planning, in May 2009, Harlem congressman Charles Rangel, New York mayor Michael Bloomberg and New York governor David Paterson joined other officials in a celebration opening the park.

Harlem fishermen at work at the West Harlem Piers Park.

Today, West Harlem Piers Park is a two-acre waterfront park with piers that accommodate various types of boating vessels, including excursion boats and water taxis, and activities ranging from fishing and water tours to boating and ecological exploration. A pedestrian and bicycle path stretches from Battery Park through Harlem and up to Dyckman Street in Washington Heights.

Tourists and Transitions

The West Harlem Piers Park waterfront has recently been developed and has quickly become a popular relaxation spot in Harlem.

Visitors to West Harlem Piers Park will see many diverse ethnic groups and families playing with children, fishermen, cyclists, walkers and skaters, among others. And when these revelers get hungry, Fairway Market is directly across the street to fill their needs. An organic and specialty market, Fairway has been serving the Harlem community for many years. Not your typical supermarket, Fairway is full of edible treats from around the world, many of which cannot easily be found elsewhere in New York City.

Marcus Garvey Memorial Park, formerly Mount Morris Park, is located along Fifth Avenue just south of 125th Street. The park is a popular meeting place for neighborhood residents to gather. The park also holds one of New York City's last remaining fire watchtowers, which were used during the late 1800s.

At the lower end of Harlem, near 110th Street and the northeast end of Central Park, sits the Harlem Meer. The Harlem Meer (between 106th Street and 110th Street, www.centralpark.com) is the second-largest man-made body of water inside of Central Park and was one of the last areas in the park to be constructed. An eleven-acre area, the Meer—which is a Dutch word meaning lake and an acknowledgement of the Dutch who settled Harlem—is a popular place for families to relax and enjoy the beautiful scenery.

HARLEM NOW

Harlem today must seem like a practically brand-new place, complete with gentrification and seemingly unstoppable development. New condos are being built; however, many remain empty. At the same time, a new upscale hotel opened, the first new hotel to open in Harlem since the Hotel Theresa closed in 1967. Harlem is changing again, and today it is a hot spot for living in New York City, as well as a hot spot for tourism. The allure that has always been part of Harlem still remains.

The Creators

A cultural breeding ground through the Harlem Renaissance years, today the community of Harlem remains an inspirational and creative force. Numerous writers, photographers and other artists have used Harlem to invigorate their creativity. Award-winning illustrator and author Colin Bootman placed his latest children's book, *The Steel Pan Man of Harlem*, in the neighborhood. The book is inspired by the Pied Piper of Hamelin and is set during the Harlem Renaissance. In his author notes, he writes:

> I chose Harlem for the setting of my story because—aside from the fact that the name sounds close to Hamelin—most Caribbean folks immigrated to Harlem during the 1920s, 1930s and 1940s. This Period was a musical time. As far as music and dance go, Harlem had a little something for everyone. Swing, the jitterbug and the samba filled the dance halls. And Caribbean immigrants introduced the celebration of Carnival.

Harlem Now

Walk or ride past any vending area in the community and you will see books by "urban writers" with stories set in Harlem. For African Americans in particular, Harlem as a community is representative of the collective black community. Although Harlem is a New York community, for African Americans, it is representative of the people at large. In Harlem, you will find black professionals and the educated, as well as those less educated. You will find your typical working-class individuals and those in need of work. And you will also find those who have lost their way and have succumbed to the societal ills that plague many urban communities across America—unemployment, drugs and crime. But in the midst of all of that, in many ways, Harlem encompasses all that is black America.

From a tourist's view, one may see the people and hustle and bustle on streets such as 116th and 125th and wonder what is going on. One may see African vendors selling incense, oils and shea butter on one table next to a young man selling CDs spread out on a cloth on the ground next to somebody else who may be holding any variety of items in their hands, attempting to sell them. And next to these people, one may see a Spanish vendor selling food from a small cart as women, men and children, young and old, walk up and down the sidewalks. Mixed in with the crowd, unknowingly to passersby,

A Harlem vendor's table on 125th Street is full of perfumed oils and African shea butter, which is used on skin and hair and comes from a tree nut in Africa.

are Harlem's working class shopping alongside Harlem's professional and middle-class citizens. This is Harlem.

While lifestyles and fashion styles may vary, everyone from the baggy pants, fitted cap and Timberland-wearing young people to the suited-down urban professionals to the poetry-loving, bohemian arts crowd, everyone here is part of the community. This is Harlem.

Duke Ellington urged us to "Take the "A" Train," and while many other subway lines run through Harlem, taking the A train still remains the most widely known way to get uptown. Perhaps the creative spirit of Ellington and his entertainment peers travels on that train. Nowadays, riders may hear a group of three or four young men clapping and suddenly announcing that it is "shooowwwtiiiimmmeee!" To a first-timer, curiosity is piqued as they observe the young men who bear no equipment, except for possibly a radio. They are not in costume, nor is their dress coordinated. Nevertheless, once "shoooowwwttiimmme" begins, most marvel at what they observe. The young men are dancers, and when they begin, they give spectacular shows of flexibility, strength and coordination. As they dance, they spin, jump, flip and swing across train poles—and they do this on trains moving at full speed!

Today, all it takes is a quick glance around the neighborhood and one can get a sense that change is going on. Construction workers line city blocks building new businesses and residences, mostly high-priced condominiums or other luxury facilities. Interestingly, as these new buildings go up, advertisements have run on the back covers of either of New York City's free daily newspapers—*AM New York* or *Metro*—advertising the lofts and "limited collection of full-floor homes" available in some of these new buildings. However, in those same advertisements, which do cite the exact street locations of the lofts or condominiums, there is no mention of Harlem. The street's location, however—138th Street, for example—puts the building squarely in Harlem. But this would only be known to those who know New York. Perhaps this is a reflection of the fact that developers know that there may still be a lingering negative perception among some people who would hesitate to consider living in Harlem. However, there are some developers who do mention the neighborhood in the ads, although it still may not be very prominent.

The future of housing is changing quickly in Harlem, with luxury buildings and condos filling up newly renovated buildings. Who occupies these buildings is a factor that is changing the demographics of Harlem day by day. While there have been a few new buildings developed in recent years in Harlem with "affordable" apartments for average citizens, much of the new development is pricey and out of range for current Harlem residents. In April 2010, one developer ran newspaper ads announcing an open house for the sale or rental of ten newly developed buildings in Harlem. With catchy building names and units full of amenities, these mostly condominium facilities range in price from $275,000 up to $1.3 million.

And because of this new development and renovation, its cultural hipness and easy accessibility to downtown Manhattan, Harlem is where people want to be. Throughout the neighborhood, one will see countless properties that have been abandoned or empty for years but are now being rejuvenated.

"Harlem has so much history, plus it's residential everywhere in Harlem. And there are so many buildings you can just go to different communities and you got family everywhere. Back in the early days with Harlem, not early days, but you know, '70s and '80s, it was mainly a black community," Forster says.

Today, that has changed.

"Yeah, like my building now. Where I live at, it looks like a frat house now because Columbia [University, www.columbia.edu] bought out a lot of residents, original residents who lived there since the building went up. Bought them out of their apartments. Some people have even lost leases due to Columbia contracts," says Forster

Columbia University, which is located on the west side of Harlem in the Morningside Heights section, has had an up-and-down relationship with the Harlem community. In recent years, it has bought numerous properties in the area, renovating and preparing them for school use. Columbia's investment in the community has caused friction with some who feel the university is buying up many of the properties in Harlem, which they fear the university will use for school purposes, ultimately pushing Harlem residents out of the community.

One sixty-two-year-old woman who has lived in Harlem for most of her life says that a lot of the changes going on in Harlem today have to do with "a lot of foreigners" moving to the area. Regarding housing development and new business, she says that the types of businesses and services being opened are "not for us," meaning the longtime residents of the community.

While the economy has been sluggish in 2009 and 2010, some projects stalled as many others are moving along. An October 2009 *New York Times* article about the former PS 90 school building in Harlem says the property, which is being developed by L+M Development Partners, will be "a mix of market-rate and moderate-income apartments." The school building has been vacant for thirty years after it was closed in the 1970s because of low enrollment. Most of the new apartments are studios and one- and two-bedroom units.

Along Broadway above 110th Street are many restaurants, bookstores, shops and large apartment buildings built before the Second World War. Columbia dominates the neighborhood, which is also the site of Barnard College, Riverside Church, Union Theological Seminary, the Bank Street College of Education, the Interchurch Center, the Goddard Institute for Space Studies and International House. Morningside Heights has a diverse population, including whites, blacks, Puerto Ricans and other Latin Americans; many residents are students and faculty members at Columbia.[75]

However, Columbia is not the only university in Harlem. Move farther uptown and you are on "CUNY turf"—the City University of New York (www.ccny.cuny.edu). Near 145th Street and Convent Avenue is where Harlem-born former secretary of state Colin Powell earned his undergraduate degree.

In September 2009, filmmaker Michael Moore screened his film *Capitalism: A Love Story* at Magic Johnson Theatres in Harlem. Imagenation (www.imagenation.us), a Harlem-based organization that promotes independent film, presented the screening. It is somewhat fitting that the film—which addresses the bank failures and rise in foreclosures that Americans have experienced in the past few years, as well as the overall greed that has been shown by large corporations through capitalism—was screened in Harlem. As Harlem changes, one thing that an observer will notice is the increase in the presence of major companies. Harlem as a community has been known to be home to smaller, more independent businesses. When looking around today, based on the businesses that are setting up shop, there is no difference in the type of businesses you will see in downtown and midtown Manhattan than in parts of Harlem.

But one interesting side note. Just a block away from where Michael Moore screened his film, which looked at how many Americans were losing their homes, nearly a whole block of Harlem stores disappeared within the last few years. This included a very popular takeout seafood restaurant that in recent years was recognized by New York's *Village Voice* as one of the city's "best affordable eats."

Nowadays in Harlem, an Old Navy, a large Foot Locker, an H&M clothing store, a Body Shop, an Aerosole shoe store and a MAC cosmetic store, among others, are side by side with discount clothing stores, African hair-braiding shops and beauty supply stores catering to African American

Harlem Now

Men on Lenox Avenue operate a vending table selling hats. Vendors work throughout the year in nearly all weather conditions.

and Latino customers. And across from them are the vendors set up on the sidewalks selling their variety of wares, books, shea butter, jewelry, CDs and countless DVDs and other material.

And new arrivals continue to make their way. In December 2009, Applebee's opened its first restaurant in Harlem at 1 West 125th Street. Just prior to that, on the east side, Costco, the big wholesale chain store, opened its doors in Harlem, but only after months of skepticism and questioning from neighboring residents. Costco is located at 517 East 117th Street in the newly developed East River Plaza in East Harlem.

As more and more chain stores fill up 125th Street, go west toward the Hudson River and you will find a newly rejuvenated entertainment hotspot. Down near 12th Avenue and Broadway, there are new clubs, restaurants, a waterfront, a specialty grocer and the newest location of the world-famous Cotton Club. The #1 train is one of the easiest ways to get here. This area is also part of the new West Harlem Pier.

The Harlem pier area is about thirty thousand square feet of space, the same stretch of land where, in the 1920s and 1930s, ferries shuttled riders back and forth to Bear Mountain and Fort Lee, New Jersey. During the 1940s and 1950s, its piers and esplanades were destroyed and left to rot.[76]

Entrance to the #1 train Harlem subway station, which is close to West Harlem Piers Park and Harlem's newly thriving entertainment area near Twelfth Avenue and Riverside Drive.

People enjoying Harlem's new waterfront area, which includes a cleaning area for fishermen and a walking and bike path.

Harlem Now

Today, the pier is a center of relaxation and fun as families gather and children play. Parents pushing baby strollers, children and adults riding bikes along the bike path, people of all ages, races and nationalities sitting on park benches facing the Hudson River, joggers trotting back and forth across the pier—all of this can be found at the Harlem Pier.

Perhaps one of the more surprising things that can be found at the pier is the fishermen's station, a built-in, open-to-anyone cleaning station where fishermen—and the pier has them—can clean their "catch of the day." When in use, the spot always attracts a lot of attention.

Dinosaur Bar-B-Que (corner of 12th Avenue and West 131st Street, 212.694.1777) was one of the first businesses in the area to jumpstart its rejuvenation. You can be blocks away and smell this famous, great-tasting barbecue cooking. Billing itself as "a genuine rib joint" with Texas-style barbecue, Dinosaur is routinely packed with a diverse clientele.

Up the street, the Hudson River Café (697 West 133rd Street, www.hudsonrivercafe.com) introduces a "soul latino" menu and offers an outside eating space where guests can enjoy the riverside action. Sleek and modern, it is one of the few, if not the only, place offering this type of menu.

Just at the corner of Twelfth Avenue and 125th Street is the current site of one of Harlem's most familiar establishments, although it is not the location where the business originated. The Cotton Club today is located at 656 West

Popular Harlem restaurant Dinosaur Bar-B-Que has earned an exceptional reputation and is part of the renewal in the West Harlem Piers Park area.

The famous Cotton Club as it appears today. Now located near the new Harlem Piers area, the nostalgia of the club still attracts thousands of visitors annually.

125th Street. The club, which originally was opened by boxer Jack Johnson under the name Club Deluxe, has gone through many changes and moves to various locations but has never lost its illustrious history and cultural allure.

When Barack Obama was elected president of the United States in January 2009, the corner of 125th and Adam Clayton Powell Boulevard once again was full of Harlemites ready to hear another politician's offerings; however, this time was different. This time, an African American was not campaigning but had won the presidential election. On a massive screen erected at the intersection, thousands watched as the newly elected president with a Harlem connection addressed the nation. According to one Harlem organization, when Barack Obama attended Columbia University, he lived on the edge of East Harlem at 339 East 94th Street between First and Second Avenues.[77]

In his book *Dreams from My Father*, Obama writes,

> *It was an uninviting block, treeless and barren, lined with soot-colored walk-ups that cast heavy shadows for the rest of the day. The apartment*

Harlem Now

was small, with slanting floors and irregular heat and a buzzer downstairs that didn't work, so that visitors had to call ahead from a pay phone at the corner gas station, where a black Doberman the size of a wolf paced through the night in vigilant patrol, its jaws clamped around an empty beer bottle.

Obama went on to talk about the presence of drug dealers in his building and other happenings that give insight into the character of the neighborhood during those years. Obama returned to Harlem in 2011 for a fundraiser at one of Harlem's hottest restaurants, Red Rooster, which is owned by celebrity chef and Harlem resident Marcus Samuelsson.

Lora Bell recalled the day after Barack Obama won the presidency and Harlem's reaction: "It was so awesome. It was so many people who came to 125th Street. So many cars was out here beeping. We had a big-screen TV outside in front of the state building. I am so happy that we got a black president and his name is Obama. I am so happy because maybe he is gonna help people out. He's gonna help." When asked what she felt Obama's win

Newspaper headlines report President Obama's historic win. President Obama lived in East Harlem while attending Columbia University.

The Harlem community supported President Obama's presidential run. These "signs of hope" Obama posters were posted at an apartment building in Harlem.

means for her four-year-old grandson as they both walked down 125th Street, she said, "That yes, he can do it. Anything he wants to do, he can do it and he don't have to have anybody telling him that he can't do it because he's a black person. Yes, we can do it."

NOTES

Introduction

1. Ellis, *Epic of New York City*, 520.
2. Wilson, *Meet Me at the Theresa*, 59.

Harlem History Since 1900

3. Osofsky, *Making of a Ghetto*, 87.
4. Ibid., 17.
5. Jackson, *Encyclopedia*, 524.
6. Osofsky, *Making of a Ghetto*, 83.
7. Ibid., 34.
8. Ibid., 88.
9. Ibid., 94.
10. Ibid., 96.
11. Jackson, *Encyclopedia*, 655.
12. Wilson, *Meet Me at the Theresa*, 56.
13. Osofsky, *Making of a Ghetto*, 172.
14. Peretti, *Lift Every Voice*, 65, 66.
15. Wilson, *Meet Me at the Theresa*, 144.
16. NYC Landmarks Preservation Commission, *Guide to New York City Landmarks*, 191.
17. Ibid., 201.
18. *New York Times*, "Only in New York," 124.

Notes

21. East Harlem Historical Organization.
22. *New York Daily News*, August 2011.
23. Wilson, *Meet Me at the Theresa*, 7.
24. www.huemanbookstore.com.
25. Wilson, *Meet Me at the Theresa*, 5.
26. Ibid., 43.
27. Smith, *Black Firsts*, 61.
28. Osofsky, *Making of a Ghetto*, 180.
29. Boyd, *Harlem Reader*, 80.
30. Smith, *Black Firsts*, 61.
31. Havelin, *Ulysses S. Grant*, 67.
32. Ibid., 73.
33. Ibid., 81.
34. Ibid., 95–96.
35. Ibid., 99.
36. Ibid., 103.
37. www.nps.gov.
38. Wilson, *Meet Me at the Theresa*, 75.
39. Kirchner, *Oxford Companion to Jazz*, 237.
40. Stone, *Up Close*, 40.
41. Peretti, *Lift Every Voice*, 97.
42. Jackson, *Encyclopedia*, 1246.
43. Larkin, 908.
44. Jackson, *Encyclopedia*, 1247.
45. *New York Daily News*, January 2, 2010.
46. Rich, *David Dinkins*, 27.
47. *New York Post*, June 26, 2009.
48. Wilson, *Meet Me at the Theresa*, 75.
49. Stone, *Up Close*, 35.
50. Wilson, *Meet Me at the Theresa*, 63.
51. Ibid., 89.
52. Williams and Rivers, *Forever Harlem*, 38.
53. Hill, *Harlem Stomp!*, 125.
54. Johnson, *Black Manhattan*.
55. Jackson, *Encyclopedia*, 1224.
56. Wintz, *Harlem Speaks*, 43.
57. Wilson, *Meet Me at the Theresa*, 64.
58. Ottley and Weatherby, *Negro in New York*, 265.
59. Greenberg, *Or Does It Explode?*, 65.

60. Wikipedia.org.
61. Ellis, *Epic of New York City*, 522.
62. Ibid.
63. www.nationalactionnetwork.net.
64. Jackson, *Encyclopedia*, 607.
65. Ibid.
66. www.clintonfoundation.org.
67. *New York Post*, December 28, 2009.
68. *New York Daily News*, December 28, 2009.

Cultural Crusades

69. Hasse, *Jazz*, 54.
70. Ibid., 57.
71. Peretti, *Lift Every Voice*, 164.

Faith and Religion in the Community

72. Johnson, *Black Manhattan*, 165.

Tourists and Transitions

73. NYC Cycling Map 2009.
74. www.h2c2harlem.com.

Harlem Now

75. Jackson, *Encyclopedia*, 771.
76. Jackson, *Harlem World*, 154–55.
77. www.harlemonestop.com.

BIBLIOGRAPHY

Boyd, Herb, ed. *The Harlem Reader*. New York: Three Rivers Press, 2003.

Ellis, Edward Robb. *The Epic of New York City*. New York: Coward McCann, 1966.

Greenberg, Cheryl Lynn. *Or Does It Explode? Black Harlem in the Great Depression*. Oxford, UK: Oxford University Press, 1991.

Hasse, John Edward, ed. *Jazz: The First Century*. New York: HarperCollins Publishers, 2000.

Havelin, Kate. *Ulysses S. Grant*. Minneapolis, MN: Lerner Publications Company, 2004.

Hill, Laban Carrick. *Harlem Stomp! A Cultural History of the Harlem Renaissance*. New York: Little Brown, 2003.

Jackson, John L., Jr. *Harlem World: Doing Race and Class in Contemporary Black America*. Chicago: University of Chicago Press, 2001.

Jackson, Kenneth T., ed. *The Encyclopedia of New York City*. New Haven, CT: Yale University Press and New York Historical Society, 2010

Johnson, James Weldon. *Black Manhattan*. New York: Da Capo Press, 1930.

Kirchner, Bill, ed. *The Oxford Companion to Jazz*. New York: Oxford University Press, 2000.

Larkin, Colin, ed. *The Virgin Encyclopedia of Jazz*. Virgin Books (UK), 2004.

New York City Landmarks Preservation Committee. *Guide to New York City Landmarks*. Third Edition. New York: John Wiley & Sons Inc., 2004.

New York Daily News, January 2, 2010.

New York Post, June 26, 2009.

NYC Cycling Map 2009.

Bibliography

Osofsky, Gilbert. Harlem: *The Making of a Ghetto, Negro New York, 1890–1930*. New York: Harper and Row, 1968.

Ottley Roi, and William J. Weatherby. *The Negro in New York: An Informal Social History*. New York: New York Public Library, 1967.

Peretti, Burton W. *Lift Every Voice: The History of African American Music*. Lanham, MD: Rowman & Littlefield Publishers Inc., 2009.

Rich, Wilbur C. *David Dinkins and New York City Politics*. New York: State University of New York Press, 2007.

The Riverside Dictionary of Biography. Boston: Houghton Mifflin Company, 2005.

Siegel, Fred. *The Prince of the City: Giuliani, New York and the Genius of American Life*. San Francisco: Encounter Books, 2005.

Smith, Jessie Carney. *Black Firsts: 4,000 Ground Breaking & Pioneering Historical Events*. Detroit: Visible Ink Press, 2003.

Stone, Tanya Lee. *Up Close: Jazz Legend Ella Fitzgerald*. New York: Viking, 2008.

Williams, Lloyd A., and Voza W. Rivers, eds. *Forever Harlem: Celebrating America's Most Diverse Community*. New York: Daily News, L.P. and the Greater Harlem Chamber of Commerce, 2006.

Wilson, Sondra Kathryn. *Meet Me at the Theresa: The Story of Harlem's Most Famous Hotel*. New York: Atria Books, 2004.

Wintz, Cary D., ed. *Harlem Speaks: A Living History of the Harlem Renaissance*. Naperville, IL: Sourcebooks, 2007.

www.east-harlem.com

ABOUT THE AUTHOR

Noreen Mallory was born in Hartford, Connecticut, and grew up in Philadelphia, Pennsylvania. She has been a staff writer and editor for a number of newspapers in Philadelphia and Boston, and her articles have appeared in various other publications.

She has also worked in television news at CNN in Atlanta and New York. She is a co-author of the book *Urban Theory: Critical Thoughts in America* and is a graduate of Harvard University.

Visit us at
www.historypress.net